Mother Angelica's

Private and Pithy Lessons
from the Scriptures

ALSO BY RAYMOND ARROYO

Mother Angelica

*Mother Angelica's Little Book of Life Lessons
and Everyday Spirituality*

Mother Angelica's

Private and Pithy Lessons
from the Scriptures

❖

Introduced and edited by

Raymond Arroyo

DOUBLEDAY

New York London Toronto Sydney Auckland

ꓦD

DOUBLEDAY

PUBLISHED BY DOUBLEDAY

Published in the United States by Doubleday, an imprint of
The Doubleday Publishing Group, a division of
Random House, Inc., New York.
www.doubleday.com

BOOK DESIGN BY AMANDA DEWEY

Library of Congress Cataloging-in-Publication Data
M. Angelica (Mary Angelica), Mother, 1923–
Mother Angelica's private and pithy lessons from the Scriptures / introduced and edited by Raymond Arroyo.
p. cm.
1. Bible—Criticism, interpretation, etc. I. Title.
BS511.3.M224 2008
220.6—dc22
2008001926

ISBN 978-0-385-51986-1

PRINTED IN THE UNITED STATES OF AMERICA

9 10

For Old Testament Rebecca
with enduring love

I went to those who were not looking for me;
I was found by those who sought me not.

—ISAIAH 65:1

Holy rusticity is better than sinful eloquence.

—SAINT JEROME

CONTENTS

Introduction

❖

For Mother Mary Angelica, it all began with the Word. And the Word was made *fresh* . . .

Everything the Poor Clare nun is known for—her television network that now reaches 140 million households around the globe, her teachings that continue to touch people throughout the world, her thriving religious orders—has its root here: in Mother Angelica's love of God's Word and the zealous, practical way she unpacked it for the common man.

Her love affair with the Scriptures began in a dramatic and unorthodox fashion. Though she had been a religious for twenty-six years, absorbing a daily diet of Scripture at Mass and through the reading of spiritual classics, she had never studied the Bible with any serious attention. Then in 1971, after repeated requests, Mother agreed to allow Father Robert DeGrandis, a charismatic Birmingham priest, to pray over her. He prayed that she would receive the "baptism of the Holy Spirit." Now, Angelica was extremely suspicious of this "baptism" and of the many charismatic Christians who espoused its virtues. These believers pursued the "gifts of the Holy Spirit": prophecy, speaking in tongues, healing powers, and so forth. They maintained that no gifts could be received without first being baptized in the Spirit. Angelica dismissed much of this talk, and only submitted herself to the laying on of hands to get Father DeGrandis to stop badgering her.

When it was over and nothing happened, she smugly stared at the priest and asked, "Is that it?" But there was more to come.

About a week later, while reading the introduction to Saint John's Gospel ("In the beginning was the Word: the Word was with God and the Word was God"), Mother found herself unable to speak English. When she tried to converse with her nuns, a language not her own spilled from her mouth. De-Grandis assured her that there was no need to worry, she had merely received the gift of tongues. The "gift" didn't last very long, but as she told me in an interview for my biography *Mother Angelica, The Remarkable Story of a Nun, Her Nerve, and a Network of Miracles,* the event had an important lasting effect on her: "I got initiated into the New Testament through this little experience . . . I think the Lord used it to reorient my soul, and the Sisters toward the Scriptures, so that we talked about them, we read them, and we discussed them. It was really the beginning."

Following this experience, Mother's daily lesson to her nuns became spirit-led riffs on the Scripture. She began to scrawl notes in the margins of her *Jerusalem Bible,* furiously underlining key passages of practical import. Soon a group of Episcopalian women asked her to lead a weekly Bible study for them, which she did. For nearly five years the Bible study in her monastery parlor became her private training ground, a place for Mother to refine her teachings before a hungry public. These "Journeys into Scripture," as she called them, became the template for her television work, and the fountainhead of the Eternal Word Television Network. Mother didn't just teach the Scriptures; she got inside them, animating them for a contemporary audience. She picked apart the stories and people of the Bible, finding humor, unexpected lessons, and punchy instruction for daily living. She made the Scriptures accessible to everyone, and somehow new again.

To truly know the Bible, there are obvious advantages to spending time with the Author. Being a contemplative nun, Mother Angelica had an inside track. She literally spent hours each day meditating and conversing with God in prayer. This daily regimen of faith is underappreciated in our age, but the benefits are enduring. Saint Teresa of Avila, the Spanish mystic, said of her experience with God during prayer: "He would take me into His room. This is a royal chamber filled with countless and immense riches. Introduced to the secrets of Heaven, like the great Saint Paul, the Bride sees invisible things and hears unutterable words." Mother Angelica saw those invisible things and heard those unutterable words as well—but unlike her contemplative peers, she was able to share the fruit of her contemplation with millions over the airwaves.

First in print, then on tape, and later on television, Mother Angelica gradually coined a theology of the street—an approach to Scripture that was immediately relatable to daily living. Rita Rizzo, as Angelica was known before religious life, came from the hard streets of southeast Canton, Ohio: an Italian ghetto, pocked with everyday struggles, heartache, and simple joys. Her painful childhood would forever connect her to the concerns of the man on the street, concerns that she brought to her exploration of the Scriptures. Mother's biblical approach, like the woman herself, was practical, no-nonsense, and very human.

Here is some useful advice Mother Angelica gave her nuns about reading the Word of God. It summarizes her philosophical approach to the Scriptures and her method for studying them:

When we read the Gospel we don't use our imaginations. We don't look at the Gospel as applicative to our lives. We look at the Gospel many times as a record of Jesus's life, a thing confined to the past. We think of it as almost a divine history book, which in a way it is. After all, this is the story of salvation history—but it is much more than that. It is a guide for living.

And we do some things wrong. We don't read enough of Scripture at one time. You go in there and pick out one little thing in isolation and don't visualize anything. It's just words. I mean, when you come across the trial and pain of Jesus we need to have an imaginative picture of that. There is a line here: "Like the sheep that is led to the slaughterhouse, like a lamb that is dumb in front of the sheers, like these He never opened His mouth." We should take that phrase and ask ourselves, "Have I ever been that frightened? Have I ever been so scared that I went dumb?" Try to imagine a time in your life when you've had that kind of fear. And dwell on the line.

"Like these, He never opened His mouth." Unlike Jesus, you're always opening your mouth about something. We're always defending ourselves. Do you see? Reading this line of Scripture you have a dual opportunity: to have sympathy for Jesus, and to examine your conscience.

There are so many ways of reading Scripture. If you're a symbolic reader, then you see symbolism in it. If you're a fundamental reader, then you take every word literally—which can be dangerous because there are contradictions. My scriptural approach is spiritual. I'm trying to apply what's here to everyday living. It's the truth. So you can't just read it like a book.

Mother sought to discover a spirituality *in* the Scriptures. Her method was earthy, relevant, and free of the stiff conventions or novel innovations that too often remove us from the core message of the Bible. Though informed by the traditions and wisdom of the Church, Angelica managed to peel back centuries of staid ideas and misunderstandings, offering us a Bible that is as current as it is funny. Here is the greatest story newly told, as only Mother Angelica can tell it.

Amazingly, Mother's Bible teachings have never been collected or arranged in print. What follows are unpublished, private Scripture lessons Angelica gave to her nuns and to small lay groups over a thirty-year stretch. You'll notice that they are far more comprehensive and detailed than the often truncated versions she delivered over the airwaves. Limitations of time and the pressures of reaching such a wide audience probably caused Mother to edit herself, and her instruction.

The teachings herein are revealing, impassioned, and startlingly personal. They come from hundreds of private audio recordings that, in collaboration with Our Lady of the Angels Monastery, I reviewed to identify those selections that most reveal Mother's originality and uncanny insight. The editing of these excerpts is intentionally light to preserve Mother Angelica's unmistakable voice. Hopscotching through the Bible, the teachings usually begin with a verse or two and quickly give way to Mother's unique running commentary. This is not your grandmother's Bible study. There are features of these unconventional reflections that set them apart from anything available:

❖ Never before have the men and women of the Bible seemed so lively, so real—so like us. Mother has a knack for exposing the humanity of these characters, and displays an intimate, at times hilarious, familiarity with them. She refers to Saint Peter as "that great bungler," Saint Paul as "the little shrimp," and of Abraham and Sarah she says: "He's ninety-nine. You can imagine what his wife looked like. Not too much sex appeal . . ."

❖ There are also several guided meditations in the pages to come. During these "Journeys into Scripture" Mother puts herself, and you, the reader, in the middle of the action. You are imaginatively "there" at key moments in the life of Christ and His apostles. In these "Journeys" she magnifies details suggested by the Scripture, and underscores key words and events most of us would breeze past. You'll notice that these teachings are in the present tense, in real time. For Mother Angelica, Jesus Christ and His message are always in the present tense, alive and moving through time.

❖ Mother Angelica poses questions directly to the reader throughout these lessons. She probes and challenges, encouraging you to take an inventory of your spiritual life at every turn. "Don't you behave the same way?" she demands at one point. When discussing the apostles battling the storm on the Sea of Galilee she asks: "What do you do when the storms are sinking your boat? When you get so frightened during life's storms, threatened, and unhappy, do you really believe that Jesus is the Son of God?" It is a direct engagement of the reader that is rarely found in any Bible study.

❖ Finally, you will discover, scattered amid the lessons, Mother's tips for reading the Scriptures and exploring them on your own.

This is your chance to have Mother Angelica personally lead you through the Bible. She jousts with the Scripture, wrestles with it at times, and gallops through the Holy Writ with an ardent abandon. It is an unpredictable journey filled with laughs and evocative surprises, but Mother's intention is to unearth the message waiting for you in the Scripture, right now. Like a prophet of old, she retreated to prayer for decades before opening her mouth to teach others. Here, in this one volume, are the fruits of her spiritual labors: her practical insights and her potent biblical reflections for you to ponder, cherish, and live.

May these lessons incite you to action—Mother would have it no other way.

RAYMOND ARROYO
June 13, 2008
Feast Day of Saint Anthony of Padua
Northern Virginia

OPENING PRAYER

Lord God and Father, we praise Thee and we bless Thee

for bringing us together today around Your Word;

For giving us Thy Son to live and to die out of love for us,

and for giving us Thy Holy Spirit to dwell within us.

And I ask, Father, that you bestow on me light and

words of wisdom. Give to each one here

what they need in body, soul, and spirit.

Search the depths of their hearts that they may find Thee,

and having found Thee, find joy—

that joy that no man can take from us.

I ask, Father, that Thy Spirit be with us, that each one here

feel Thy Holy Spirit in the very depths of their souls.

I ask Thy paternal blessing.

Amen.

Meditating on the Scriptures
with Mother Angelica

❖

A Primer

Most of us meditate on things totally useless to the spiritual life. Those who say they "can't" often meditate the most. Their minds get stuck on one thing and they mull it over and over. They're meditating a lot—on the wrong things! Don't tell me you don't know how to meditate. When you get angry with someone you can meditate on that for at least half a day, can't you? When you're upset it can consume you for the other half of the day. We review our lives like scenes in a play. You remember what that one said and what the other one said and then you add more to it. You not only meditate, but you use your imagination. We all go through a series of thoughts and imaginings. The essence of the interior life is to control that and focus it on God. We're all massive meditators. We just need to keep focused on God and learn what to meditate on.

I want to begin our lesson with what we call scriptural meditation. If you don't meditate when you read Scripture, you won't get the point. You're reading it like a newspaper. Scriptural meditation is really easy.

In every meditation you must do two things: you must use your memory (to express what you already know) and you must use your imagination. If one of those is missing, you are not meditating. . . . Some Christians read Scripture to memorize it, and every week they commit a passage to memory, but we need to read Scripture as a meditation. Now, you can read it paragraph by paragraph, but if you don't meditate on it, it won't stick to the mind and the heart. And you can have a lot of fun with the Scriptures. I hope your meditations are gleeful, fun, and moving. The more you meditate, the more you begin to see how the human and divine are so close, in your soul especially—because your soul was created by God and for God.

I've opened up to the beginning of Mark, chapter 8, and the reason Mark is a good gospel to meditate on is because he has a lot of detail that the other evangelists don't have. It's easier to meditate if we have detail. This is the miracle of the loaves.

It says: AND NOW ONCE AGAIN A GREAT CROWD HAD GATHERED. Now don't rush on. You've got to stop and *see* a great crowd. They may be coming down from a mountain. They may be coming up from the seashore. They may have been on the road and heard the Master is on the hill and have run over. In this short paragraph, your imagination can engage and suddenly you have a picture, a beautiful picture of something happening in the life of Jesus.

AND [THEY HAD] NOTHING TO EAT. Now ask yourself: why? A great crowd had gathered, and you can see that great crowd on a little tiny mountain or knoll, and all these people are there. You can see some sitting, some standing, some talking, and there's a lull, and they're hungry. They were so enthralled with Jesus that they forgot to eat. They didn't even think of food. Now you have planted in your memory a little seed from your imagination. And we're only one sentence in.

SO HE CALLED HIS DISCIPLES TO HIM. Now, there again, wait and see the scene in your imagination. You can see the apostles, and the Lord saying, "Psst, come here Peter, I want to talk to you all a minute." And they wander over from here and there. What do they look like? Do they immediately listen to the Lord? Now, don't say to me, "I can't do that." Oh, yeah? You meditate from the time you get up till the time you go to bed on silly things. Pull it together and meditate on holy things! Now you can see Our Lord calling these apostles and in your mind, if you're meditating you see something new, and you wonder, *wonder,* what is He going to tell them? What's He going to do? Is He going to dismiss the crowd? What's He going to do? Then, you go to the next sentence and He says, "I FEEL SORRY FOR ALL THESE PEOPLE" (8:2). Wow. See, you could stop there and think, "Wow. He feels sorry for me too." He has to. He feels very sorry for me, too, because I hunger and thirst for God, for holiness of life. He knew about the needs of the people. The apostles didn't know. Isn't that strange? Not one of them had gone up to Him and said, "Master, they're all hungry. It's suppertime."

He said, "THEY HAVE BEEN WITH ME FOR THREE DAYS." Think of that. Don't just go over "for three days da-da-lee-dee-dah." Have you ever been so immersed in anything for three days? No. We are always immersed in ourselves, not for three days but for weeks and months that's all we can think about—our past, our future, tomorrow, the next day. We're immersed in ourselves. But many of these people had never seen or heard Jesus before, so they are in a state of astonishment. Because when He spoke, something went through them. They were so immersed in Him, that for three days they didn't even think, "Hey, I didn't eat today."

[THEY HAD] NOTHING TO EAT (8:2). Now, Jesus is thinking before He called the apostles, "IF I SEND THEM OFF HOME HUNGRY THEY WILL COLLAPSE ON THE WAY" (8:3). He knew that hunger made them weak, but they never complained. Do you see how attentive Jesus is to our concerns, our needs? Hasn't Jesus known you your whole life? Hasn't He cared for you every moment, guiding events in your life? If He let you go one way or another, you might have lost your soul—or your mission. Think of that. Now, you're beginning to get a picture of the personality of Jesus. He's awesome and totally selfless.

This is why I like Saint Mark for meditation. "SOME HAVE COME A GREAT DISTANCE" (8:3), the Lord says. They may have walked a hundred miles, twenty miles, and then sat there for three days without food. You want to know Jesus? Think of that. I don't know anybody at all—Bishop Sheen could hold people for an hour—but there aren't many who can hold people's attention beyond that. The Lord did for three days. Now you're beginning to understand something about Jesus.

You're going to be shocked because His disciples said, "WHERE COULD ANYONE GET BREAD TO FEED THESE PEOPLE IN A DESERTED PLACE LIKE THIS?" (8:4). Now, you can see yourself in that. Stop at this point and think: Where could anyone get bread to feed these people in this desert place? Haven't you made excuses sometimes when God asks you to do something? Haven't you and I said, "No, this is impossible. I can't do that. This is a desert. I don't have the strength. I can't do it." Oh, listen. If you want an examination of conscience, this one sentence will do it for you. That's what a meditation does: it brings the worst out of you so you can compare it to perfection.

Without meditating on the Scriptures, you're not going to get a thing out of them. Oh, you'll get something because it's the Word of God, and the Word of God is powerful, but if you don't use the faculties He has given you, you will be missing the big picture: a clear image of Him and His compassion.

Did you notice that He let them *wait three days?* They were hungry the first day, they were hungrier the second day, and they were ravenous the third day. So you find in Our Jesus a personality that's so unique. He acts the same way with you and me. When He doesn't answer our prayers, He lets us hunger a day. When He doesn't do what we desire, He lets us hunger a second day. And when we're dissatisfied with His will, He makes us wait a third day in hunger and thirst until the time comes when He decides He has to help us. How's that for a meditation, sweetheart?

> *A man who is well grounded in the testimonies of the Scripture is the bulwark of the Church.*
>
> — SAINT JEROME

The Old Testament

In the Beginning

❖

Genesis 1:1–31

Today as we begin our Bible study, we start with the book of Genesis. The first four books of the Bible are attributed to Moses, but scholars have discovered that there are different forms and traditions of these books: the Yahwehist tradition, the Eloist tradition, the Deuteronomist tradition. Men of different times added and at times repeated things. There are no myths in the Scripture, but there are stories and legends. In order to reveal to finite minds something of the beauty of God and creation, we now have a written account—but we must remember as we read this that the Word was passed on orally for many, many centuries. Some think that Scripture is as old as creation. Moses merely wrote what had been passed down for generations, thousands of years perhaps—who knows. For the sake of future generations, Moses began to put down in writing the marvels that God had worked. So we have the book of Genesis. In the beginning . . . (1:1).

Now when you read Scripture, you must first of all read it as a prayer. It is more than a historical document. It is revelation. We as finite creatures have no concept of God, His love, His mercy, or His forgiveness. This book is a revelation of how much God loves you. You must read it slowly, as a prayer, and you must read it with your imagination.

Never read Scripture unless you engage your mental faculties: your memory, your understanding, and your will. Now

I want you to do this: as I read the Scripture and comment upon it I want you to picture the entire scene in your mind. And when you read Scripture alone, you must see a picture. You've got to use your mental faculties. The best way to read Scripture is to put yourself in that time. I keep telling you that to God all things are present, so that when you read IN THE BEGINNING . . . you are there. Why? Because you were present in the mind of God then! Very often today people say the Scriptures are not relevant. That is not true. Scripture is relevant every day: in the past and in the future. It is because you do not read Scripture properly that you cannot take the nitty-gritty of this day. You can't accept life with its heartaches and problems and mysteries—mysteries that can never be solved, only accepted. Scripture is not something you're going to understand fully. For all eternity we will contemplate and meditate on those first words of Genesis: IN THE BEGINNING GOD CREATED THE HEAVENS AND THE EARTH.

You know, if you use your imagination you can hardly get past that one sentence. Can you imagine going back to a time when there was nothing, absolutely nothing? You cannot imagine nothing, because everything you've ever encountered is *something*.

The Scripture says: IN THE BEGINNING . . . You can just about feel the utter silence of nothing. IN THE BEGINNING GOD CREATED THE HEAVENS AND THE EARTH. NOW THE EARTH WAS A FORMLESS VOID, THERE WAS DARKNESS OVER THE DEEP, AND GOD'S SPIRIT HOVERED OVER THE WATER (1:2). Isn't that a meditation? Can you imagine just for a moment—just block everything out of your mind for a moment—and put yourself in the past, at the beginning. That same Spirit that lives in you hovered over the water.

Then we like to imagine the voice of God, like thunder,

coming out of nothingness and announcing: "LET THERE BE LIGHT," AND THERE WAS LIGHT (1:3). From nothing to light. And GOD SAW THAT LIGHT WAS GOOD, AND GOD DIVIDED LIGHT FROM DARKNESS (1:4). Scholars tell us that this might reference the creation of the angels. The angelic spirit world is pure spirit, pure light. Later on it speaks about the sun and the moon, and many have wondered why He would create the sun and the moon when He had already said, "LET THERE BE LIGHT." God separated light from darkness, the good angels from the bad. I like to think of it that way—He created the magnificent spirit world of pure intelligence.

The Scripture says, GOD CALLED LIGHT "DAY", AND DARK-NESS HE CALLED "NIGHT". EVENING AND MORNING CAME: THE FIRST DAY (1:5). Now this may have taken millions of years.

There is nothing in Scripture against evolution, so long as you recognize that God is the Prime Mover. Although in my ignorant mind I've often wondered, "Why are there still apes around if we came from them?" Somewhere along the line if apes became man, wouldn't all the apes be men by now? It's just a question. Maybe it comes from not being too bright, but I'm happier this way. . . . And this "random selection" stuff is wacko. There is nothing random about the designs of God. But let's get back to Genesis.

So GOD SAID, "LET THERE BE A VAULT IN THE WATERS TO DIVIDE THE WATERS IN TWO." AND SO IT WAS (1:6). GOD MADE THE VAULT, AND IT DIVIDED THE WATERS ABOVE THE VAULT FROM THE WATERS UNDER THE VAULT (1:7). GOD CALLED THE VAULT "HEAVEN." EVENING CAME AND MORNING CAME: THE SECOND DAY (1:8).

Now some of our intellectual brethren will say to you, "You don't really believe that? From nothing comes nothing." Only God can create. Only God by a sheer act of His will can create. And whether that creation took one day or a billion days or a billion years, it doesn't matter. It is still the work of a Superior Being—God, creating out of nothing. As you read this you must realize that you were in God's mind when He created that vault and the waters under heaven. You want to read this book of Genesis with feeling. You want to read it with your imagination and with yourself present in the mind of God.

I am often accused of not being realistic, of having my mind in the heavens and never dealing with nitty-gritty living—but you know, *this* is real. To live knowing that I was in God's mind when He made that vault and the dry land, it makes this rat race world livable. This is real. God's creation is real.

GOD SAID, "LET THERE BE LIGHTS IN THE VAULT OF HEAVEN TO DIVIDE DAY FROM NIGHT (1:14), . . . TO SHINE ON THE EARTH." AND SO IT WAS (1:15). GOD MADE THE TWO GREAT LIGHTS: THE GREATER LIGHT TO GOVERN THE DAY, THE SMALLER LIGHT TO GOVERN THE NIGHT, AND THE STARS (1:16). GOD SET THEM IN THE VAULT OF HEAVEN TO SHINE ON THE EARTH (1:17), TO GOVERN THE DAY AND THE NIGHT AND TO DIVIDE LIGHT FROM DARKNESS. GOD SAW THAT IT WAS GOOD (1:18). EVENING CAME AND MORNING CAME: THE FOURTH DAY (1:19). I think it gives glory to God, because He is infinite, there is no limit to His power. You see, He created this little bitty thing and then, boom, He creates the whole thing.

This book of Genesis is so fantastic when you use your imagination a little bit. The Spirit in you should come in contact with the Spirit in this book so that you can understand something of the mystery within it. How does this relate to you? This is important. The creation of the world must relate to your life. For those of us who are not theologians, we who eat and drink and work, it isn't important how high Mount Sinai is or what they ate in the time of Abraham or what the land looked like. Those things are good information, but for you it is only important that you read Scripture with the mind of God, with great love and affection.

GOD SAID, "LET THE EARTH PRODUCE EVERY KIND OF LIVING CREATURE: CATTLE, REPTILES, AND EVERY KIND OF WILD BEAST (1:24). . . . LET US MAKE MAN IN OUR OWN IMAGE, IN THE LIKENESS OF OURSELVES, AND LET THEM BE MASTERS OF THE FISH OF THE SEA, THE BIRDS OF HEAVEN, THE CATTLE, ALL THE WILD BEASTS AND ALL THE REPTILES THAT CRAWL UPON THE EARTH" (1:26). . . . MALE AND FEMALE GOD CREATED THEM. GOD BLESSED THEM, SAYING TO THEM, "BE FRUITFUL, MULTIPLY, FILL THE EARTH AND CONQUER IT" (1:27). This is important.

So many people think the original sin was sex—obviously not, because the Lord told them to "be fruitful and multiply." The forbidden fruit was pride, as it is today. Pride: "No one will tell me what to do." AND GOD SAID, "SEE, I GIVE YOU ALL THE SEED-BEARING PLANTS THAT ARE UPON THE WHOLE EARTH, AND ALL THE TREES WITH SEED-BEARING FRUIT; THIS SHALL BE YOUR FOOD (1:29). TO ALL WILD BEASTS, ALL BIRDS OF HEAVEN AND ALL LIVING REPTILES ON THE EARTH I GIVE ALL THE FOLIAGE OF PLANTS FOR FOOD." AND SO IT WAS (1:30). GOD SAW ALL HE HAD MADE, AND INDEED IT WAS VERY GOOD. EVENING CAME AND MORNING CAME: THE SIXTH DAY (1:31).

You know we have a lesson here: God created the world, He created Adam and Eve. He gave them the world to use; to feed them, to clothe them, to make them happy, to delight in, to walk with God in. They received preternatural gifts: to live without pain, without sorrow, without heartache. Imagine that. They were endowed with a deep intelligence. There was no death. The world could feed them till their fill without toil. These are things Adam and Eve had. We don't know how long they had them. So often in life we strive for things, we exert a lot of effort and work and sweat, and when we get those things, they turn to ashes. They're gone. Then you ask, "Why did I work so hard? What was I looking for?" Maybe Adam and Eve were that way. Maybe they got tired of the abundance of God's gifts. Being grateful for all He gives us is the better path.

The Fall

❖

Genesis 3:1–12

Saint Padre Pio was once asked what he thought the greatest sin in the world was today. He said curiosity. I would have chosen at least three or four bigger ones, but he got to the root of everything. Look at how the devil deals with Adam and Eve. He comes as a serpent.

A lot of people today say, "Aw, that's kind of a story, serpents don't talk." Why do we like to split hairs like they did in seventeenth-century parlors? They used to discuss and fight over religious matters. So here comes the serpent (story or not, let's not split hairs; let's get to the point): IT ASKED THE WOMAN, "DID GOD REALLY SAY YOU WERE NOT TO EAT FROM ANY OF THE TREES IN THE GARDEN?" (3:1). THE WOMAN ANSWERED THE SERPENT, "WE MAY EAT THE FRUIT OF THE TREES IN THE GARDEN" (3:2). Now that was her first mistake: she opened her big mouth, which should teach us a lesson. Don't talk to the devil. Don't even answer him. She made her first mistake. She continued: "BUT OF THE FRUIT OF THE TREE IN THE MIDDLE OF THE GARDEN, GOD SAID, 'YOU MUST NOT EAT IT, NOR TOUCH IT

UNDER PAIN OF DEATH' " (3:3). THEN THE SERPENT SAID TO THE WOMAN, "NO! YOU WILL NOT DIE! (3:4). GOD KNOWS IN FACT THAT ON THE DAY YOU EAT IT YOUR EYES WILL BE OPENED AND YOU WILL BE LIKE GODS, KNOWING GOOD AND EVIL" (3:5).

Her second mistake was that she listened to the enemy. The first thing she did was to hear his voice and answer. The second problem was: she listened. THE WOMAN SAW THAT THE TREE WAS GOOD TO EAT AND PLEASING TO THE EYE, AND THAT IT WAS DESIRABLE FOR THE KNOWLEDGE THAT IT COULD GIVE. SO SHE TOOK SOME OF ITS FRUIT AND ATE IT. SHE GAVE SOME ALSO TO HER HUSBAND WHO WAS WITH HER, AND HE ATE IT (1:6). Gullible!

The devil essentially asks Eve (and I'm paraphrasing), "Can you eat from that tree?"

She said, "Oh, no, we're not permitted to eat from that tree."

"Why?"

"Well, the Lord God said we couldn't."

"Oh, I know why He said that."

"Why?" (Here we go.)

"Because if you eat from it, you'll be like God. You'll know good from evil." (Whenever you read the word "know" in Scripture, it means "experience." It doesn't mean the acquisition of knowledge. It means experience.)

Eve says, "Really?"

"Oh yeah. You'll have something you never had before," the serpent says.

"Wow." (I'm ad-libbing a little bit here.)

Then perhaps he said, "You know, I think God's very unfair to forbid you from eating of that tree. It's beautiful to behold and it's in your garden. Doesn't make much sense that you can't eat from it." Something convinced her, and I can only imagine that her curiosity got the best of her. Then he would have said, "Well, go on, try it."

So there she is, crunching away. It must have tasted good. If it hadn't she would have thrown it down and said something like, "I can see why the Lord God told us not to eat from that one." But she didn't; it tasted very good and very different from any other fruit. Then I would think Adam comes along and probably yells at her: "What are you doing?"

And she said, "It's very good, and it isn't at all like the Lord God said it was."

"Really?"

"No." See the curiosity coming along throughout the whole thing? There's an insatiable curiosity in spite of everything they had been given, all the gifts they had. Which proves to me that all our bellyaching about the things we want from God, and the good things we "need," and the comfortable "necessities," and all the rest would not solve the problems we have. It didn't for Adam and Eve—and we can't even imagine what they had.

The first thing they did after the fall was to hide from God. They were afraid. The first sign of disobedience to God's will is fear. What does Adam say when God finds him? "I WAS AFRAID BECAUSE I WAS NAKED, SO I HID," (3:10), Adam says. He'd been walking around naked since his creation. He didn't go around looking for big leaves before that.

And the Lord said, "WHO TOLD YOU THAT YOU WERE NAKED? . . . HAVE YOU BEEN EATING OF THE TREE I FORBADE YOU TO EAT?" (3:11).

THE MAN REPLIED, "IT WAS THE WOMAN YOU PUT WITH ME; SHE GAVE ME THE FRUIT, AND I ATE IT" (3:12).

The second sign of disobedience is a failure to take personal responsibility for your actions. What he should have said was, "Eve was tempted and she gave me the fruit and I had an idea that I could resist. But I couldn't resist, and I fell." That would have been an honest answer. But he didn't say that, and neither do we. Today if you're feeling angry, or guilty—who do you blame? Yourself? No. It's always so-and-so. It's this situation. This is unfair. This is unjust. It's never you.

After Adam and Eve disobeyed God, they excused themselves. The sad thing is, they knew they should not listen to this enemy. They had no ignorance. They knew that this creature was evil. It wasn't a surprise. The excuse was an excuse: "he tempted me." But if you have clarity of mind and you still give in to temptation, that's the recipe for a mortal sin. Adam and Eve had clarity. They knew. Now, I don't know if they knew the consequences of their sin for all generations—we don't know that—but we do know that when they sinned they had clarity of mind and absolutely no ignorance. God said, "no," and they ignored Him. They even knew why He said no. Still they made the bad choice. And we do that each time we sin.

Where Are You?

❖

Genesis 3:9, 13

After Adam and Eve chow down on that fruit and sew themselves some outfits, the Lord comes along and says, "WHERE ARE YOU? (3:9) . . . WHAT IS THIS YOU HAVE DONE?" (3:13).

So here are Adam and Eve who sinned and sorrowfully disappointed the Lord. He says, "Where are you?" How many times does Our Lord perhaps say that to you? Where are you? Where are you in your thoughts? Where are you in your desires? Where are you in your hopes? Where are you in faith and hope and love? Where are you? Where are you in your love for your neighbor, for the world, for mankind? Where are you?

We have to be careful we don't say what Adam said: "I heard your voice and I hid myself because I was afraid." We must never be afraid of the voice of God. The only reason Adam and Eve began to have fear is they did something they shouldn't have. And as we live, we have to respond to God's forgiveness with total acceptance.

It's an amazing phenomenon how many people live in the past. We call it scrupulosity, but it's an evil because it questions the wisdom, the forgiveness, and the mercy of an infinite God—which makes no sense at all. We're not responding, you see, to His mercy. We always think, "I'm outside of it," or "It's too much," or "I did something so terrible." We get so stuck on our failures. God calls and we hide ourselves like Adam did. "I heard Your voice and I hid because I was naked."

If I am doing the will of God, I don't ever need to hide. Never. What makes us hide from God is our unwillingness to accomplish His Holy Will—and so we're like Adam. For what reason? Because you're a sinner? No. We're all sinners. What we're saying is my finite sin is beyond the infinity of God's mercy, and so I hide myself. Peter said that. He said, "Depart from me, for I am a sinful man oh Lord" (Lk 5:8). At least he knew where he was. But you never see Peter getting out of the boat and running away from Jesus. He knows where he's safe, and he slowly begins to wish only to do the will of God.

Walking with God

❖

Genesis 3:8; 5:24

THE MAN AND HIS WIFE HEARD THE SOUND OF YAHWEH GOD WALKING IN THE GARDEN IN THE COOL OF THE DAY (3:8). Now some theologians will come along and say, "God didn't do that." Oh forget it, will ya! *You* walk in the garden with God in the cool of the day. This poetic imagery is there for a purpose, for you to use your imagination, for you to understand the closeness of God. So don't get all caught up in "was there a cool of the day?" and "did God come down?"

You can't imagine walking with God at twilight, can you? In the Scriptures Adam is so laid-back about the whole thing: "Oh, hi, God. Nice to see You this evening." You wonder, did they talk to God like that? What was God's relationship with Adam like? Adam walked with God every evening, and they must have talked about a lot of things since everything was just beginning at that point. I bet He'd say to Adam, "Look, I've got something new for you. Look at this. What do you want to call it?" What fun. It must have been just a delightful, delightful experience.

Scripture tells us that ENOCH WALKED WITH GOD (5:24). So did Noah. You and I must also walk with God in our hearts, in our minds, in our thoughts. When we walk with God it means He is our hope, He is our love. For Him we do everything. For Him we endure everything. For Him we look for everything. We can walk with God just as these Old Testament figures did, today, at every moment.

In God's Time

❖

Genesis 15:2–6

When Abraham was ninety years old the Lord said, "You're going to have a son," and his wife Sarah just laughed. I mean she's probably ninety-two or ninety-three. Well, you would think if God Almighty came down here and said, "You're going to have something you've always wanted," that it would happen tomorrow, right? Wrong! Nine years pass. By this time, Abraham is really old and wrinkled and he's just out of it. He's ninety-nine. You can imagine what his wife looked like. Not too much sex appeal, I would imagine. And the Lord comes back again and He says, "You will have a son." So Sarah decides to use her head. She thinks: "Well, I'm going to help God with this little prophecy." So she tells Abraham one day, "I'm sick of waiting. Here's my handmaid. Have a son with her and that will be mine." Sorry—didn't work! As soon as the handmaid got pregnant Sarah was jealous. Messed the whole thing up.

That's where we don't understand God and we don't understand faith. Like Abraham and Sarah, we expect our circumstances to be absolutely perfect and then we will practice faith. You don't need faith in perfect circumstances. Our whole concept of how God should exercise us in faith, hope, and love is so screwed up that there's no way for us to practice these great virtues.

Meanwhile, Abraham still believes it's going to happen and it does. He finally has a son by Sarah. The boy grows to be about twelve years old and the Lord says, "I want you to make a little sacrifice. I want you to sacrifice your son." Can you imagine the Lord asking you to sacrifice your only son after waiting for ninety-nine years? So he drags the boy up a mountain, puts him on a rack, and prepares to sacrifice him. I don't know anyone who would do that, including myself. The Lord is demanding. But, you see, if we don't trust Him, we will never know what He wants of us. God did not intend to take that boy's life, but he did push Abraham far enough to determine how much he loved God. How much do you love God? How far are you willing to go for Him?

In the Old Testament these men and women were tried sorely. In your life too the circumstances may not seem to be conducive to faith. But those are the circumstances for faith. Faith shows itself in darkness, not in light. If you have light then you don't need faith or hope—you have it! The beauty of practicing faith is to do so when we have absolutely no reason to believe. God comes in His own time, not ours. Just when everything seems impossible, God's time arrives and we see clearly. But without perseverance, there's no light at the end of the tunnel. No light at all. So you have to realize: circumstances that exercise our faith are often vastly different from what we expect or would like. Just ask Abraham.

Mission and Imperfections

❖

Exodus 3:7, 10–17; 4:10–16

God says to Moses in Exodus, "I HAVE SEEN THE MISERABLE STATE OF MY PEOPLE . . . [AND] HEARD THEIR APPEAL . . . I AM WELL AWARE OF THEIR SUFFERINGS" (3:7). This is a marvelous paragraph. Sometimes you look around and you pray and you pray and nothing seems to change. And you have the sneaking suspicion that the Lord went out to lunch somewhere and never came back. You just wonder, "Does He really know me? Does He understand what I'm suffering?" Most of our problems are really little, you know. But they are big to us. A child whose little sand castle has been trampled on by some big adult cries and cries, and we say, "Oh, what's a sand castle?" But it means a lot to him. And this should give you a spirit of empathy for your neighbor, because what your neighbor suffers may be very small to you, very insignificant, but as long as it causes him pain, you should have some kind of sympathy. We need to see the sufferings of other people just as God saw the sufferings of His people.

The Lord then tells Moses that He wants him to go see the Pharaoh (Ex 3:10). Do you know what Moses answers? He says, "WHO AM I TO GO TO PHARAOH AND BRING THE SONS OF ISRAEL OUT OF EGYPT?" (3:11). And God says, "I SHALL BE WITH YOU. . . . AND THIS IS THE SIGN BY WHICH YOU SHALL KNOW THAT IT IS I WHO HAVE SENT YOU. . . . AFTER YOU HAVE LED THE PEOPLE OUT OF EGYPT, YOU ARE TO OFFER WORSHIP TO GOD ON THIS MOUNTAIN" (3:12). Moses does something here that most of us do, and I've done it myself many times. You get an inspiration and you look at it and you think, "Well, this is good, this must be from the Lord." And then you proceed to argue with yourself. You argue with God and you say, "Nah. Why would He want me to do that? What's He going to do with all these spiritual booklets? Why should I do anything? Why would He want me to start a TV network?" Arguing with God. That's what we do.

Then Moses said to God, "I am to go, then, to the sons of Israel and say to them, 'the God of your fathers has sent me to you.' But if they ask me what his name is, what am I to tell them?" (3:13). And God said to Moses, "I Am who Am" (3:14). Do you know what that means? Eternal. I Am Who Am. It means that God has no beginning and no end.

And Moses gets together all the people of Israel and he says, "God . . . has appeared to me. . . . and he has said to me: . . . I have resolved to bring you up out of Egypt" (3:16–17). You know, what would happen if you went to any of your friends and said, "The Lord God has appeared to me." Ha ha ha. They would without a doubt say, "You know, I would look in the yellow pages under 'psychiatrist' and pick one out for yourself." These Israelites were no different. Now what would you do if the Lord came to you and said all this? Do you think you'd be encouraged at this point? No? Moses looks at God, and he says, "But, my Lord, never in my life have I been a man of eloquence, either before or since you have spoken to your servant" (4:10). You know what he's saying to God: "Even with all this vision and stuff, I haven't improved a bit. I stuttered before I saw You and I'll stutter after." Sometimes we're like that with the Lord. We think, here I have found the Lord, and I really want to be good, I want to be a Christian, I want to be perfect, I want to be holy—and we find more imperfections in ourselves than in anyone else. My friend who knows I want to be good says to me, "You were better before you were a Christian." Or they look at you and say, "Ha ha, look at the Christian, so impatient, so unkind, so irritable." I wouldn't feel bad. At least you're trying.

Then Moses continues: "I AM A SLOW SPEAKER AND NOT ABLE TO SPEAK WELL" (4:11). And Yahweh said, "WHO GAVE MAN HIS MOUTH? . . . WHO MAKES HIM DUMB OR DEAF, GIVES HIM SIGHT OR LEAVES HIM BLIND? IS IT NOT I, YAHWEH? (4:11). NOW GO, I SHALL HELP YOU TO SPEAK AND TELL YOU WHAT TO SAY" (4:12). Wouldn't you think *now* Moses would be kind of encouraged and say, "Alright, I do stutter; but you know when I get up there I'm not going to stutter. I have that much confidence in the Lord." Do you know what Moses says? (He not only stutters, he's stubborn too.) "IF IT PLEASES YOU, MY LORD"—at least he's polite—"SEND ANYONE YOU WILL!" (4:13). AT THIS, THE ANGER OF YAHWEH BLAZED OUT AGAINST MOSES, AND HE SAID TO HIM, "THERE IS YOUR BROTHER AARON THE LEVITE. . . . I KNOW THAT HE IS A GOOD SPEAKER (4:14). . . . YOU WILL SPEAK TO HIM AND TELL HIM WHAT MESSAGE TO GIVE (4:15). . . . HE HIMSELF IS TO SPEAK TO THE PEOPLE IN YOUR PLACE; HE WILL BE YOUR MOUTHPIECE, AND YOU WILL BE AS THE GOD INSPIRING HIM" (4:16). You know, the absolute beautiful mercy of the Father is just tremendous here. Moses is a man who absolutely refused to submit to the Lord's designs, the great lawgiver. The man who was so holy he had to veil his face from the Israelites. The people couldn't stand looking at the brilliance of his face. Yet he was full of imperfections. He lacked faith. He lacked trust in God.

You know, I think he made himself more ridiculous doing it his way. Because when he gets up there before Pharaoh, what happens? He has to whisper to his brother the entire time, prompting him to speak. Aaron's there leaning over, listening to Moses before he can say one word to Pharaoh. I imagine Pharaoh must have watched this and said, "Look at these two crazies." All this because Moses didn't trust the Lord.

You and I in our particular life, in our quest for holiness and union with God, must not be discouraged and we must learn to trust God. You have a Father who understands you perfectly. He understood Moses here. And even though Moses was obstinate, God did not take his first mission from him. His mission was to speak to the people—whether he did it himself or through someone else, he would do it, and no one else would do it.

So if you're being called by the Lord, you have a mission. You'll either accomplish it, or God will accomplish it through you regardless of your faults and your imperfections. He will do it. Because it is not your holiness; it is God in you Who is holy. Moses had to appreciate his own imperfections to keep him humble. This gave him a depth of humility that permitted God to use him to do great things. That's how God is going to treat you. He loves you, He knows you, He knows your faults, your weaknesses, He knows your circumstances, He knows everything there is to know about you. And if He has placed His hand on you, He will take care of you.

The idea here is that sometimes in life we ask God for things, and we seem to get just the opposite in reply. But that is exactly when our trust in God must be strong, because God has a purpose. He sees the whole chapter; the whole plan is in His mind. You just see the beginning. He sees the whole thing. All we have to do is to continue to pray as Moses prayed. He had doubts. He went to the Lord many times and said, "What are you doing? You tell me to do one thing and I do it and it brings more consternation and confusion and heartache upon this people. Help me!" (Ex 5:22–23; 10:18). And he'd go back again and things got worse—but he *went*. You see, the thing about Moses is, that he kept doing God's will, regardless of how bad things were or looked. He kept on praying, he kept on doing His will. He did not understand but he was obedient. I think that's the most beautiful lesson that this whole book of Exodus has to offer. It shows not only God's mercy and God's providence and God's love for His people, but it also shows Moses's faith. In darkness, in confusion, in obscurity, in anxiety, in the midst of tension, he continued to pray, he continued to do God's will even though he did not see the light at the end of the tunnel, and he kept moving forward.

Permitting Tragedies

❖

Exodus 11:9; 12:5–6, 11

Then came that memorable night when God said, "PHARAOH WILL NOT LISTEN TO YOU (11:9). . . . THIS MONTH IS TO BE THE FIRST OF ALL THE OTHERS FOR YOU, THE FIRST MONTH OF YOUR YEAR. . . . ON THE TENTH DAY OF THIS MONTH EACH MAN MUST TAKE AN ANIMAL FROM THE FLOCK (12:1–3). . . . IT MUST BE AN ANIMAL WITHOUT BLEMISH, A MALE ONE YEAR OLD (12:5). . . . YOU MUST KEEP IT TILL THE FOURTEENTH DAY OF THE MONTH . . . SLAUGHTER IT (12:6). . . . SOME OF THE BLOOD MUST THEN BE TAKEN AND PUT ON THE TWO DOORPOSTS AND THE LINTEL OF THE HOUSES (12:7). . . . DO NOT EAT ANY OF IT RAW OR BOILED, BUT ROASTED OVER THE FIRE, HEAD, FEET AND ENTRAILS (12:9). . . . YOU SHALL EAT IT HASTILY: IT IS A PASSOVER IN HON-

OUR OF YAHWEH (12:11). THAT NIGHT, I WILL GO THROUGH THE
LAND OF EGYPT AND STRIKE DOWN ALL THE FIRST-BORN IN THE
LAND OF EGYPT, MAN AND BEAST ALIKE" (12:12).

Now I know some of you ask, Why would God do such
a thing? If Pharaoh had listened in the first place, none of
this would have happened. The same thing happens in our
lives. God may be calling some people to real conversion, to
a real change of life. He calls them very quietly at first. But
they won't listen. Then His voice gets stronger and they still
won't listen. And if He loves them very much (and He does),
sometimes He will permit tragedies in their lives—permit, not
ordain, permit tragedies—in order to make them understand
the one thing necessary: to follow God.

He is a gentle God, a loving God. If you just listen to His
voice the first time it is always better. He will follow you until
you die. He will continue to reach out to you and hover over
you and wait longingly for your love, your attention, your devotion, your adoration, your praise, and your thanksgiving.

Trusting God

❖

Numbers 14:3–31

After going into the Promised Land, Caleb returns to Moses and the Israelites and announces that it is time to go
into the land. But others were fearful and worried that the risk
was just too high.

What did they do?

They began to murmur again. They said, "WHY DOES
YAHWEH BRING US TO THIS LAND, ONLY TO HAVE US FALL BY

THE SWORD, AND OUR WIVES AND YOUNG CHILDREN SEIZED AS BOOTY?" (14:3). . . . LET US APPOINT A LEADER AND GO BACK TO EGYPT" (14:4). Now they're ready to get rid of Moses and to get rid of Aaron. Isn't it fantastic how we can see the error in other people's lives but not in our own? Are we under some illusion that we don't do the same thing when we are faced with the slightest challenge or resistance to our plans? Do you think human nature has changed in the least? It hasn't.

BEFORE THE WHOLE ASSEMBLED COMMUNITY OF THE SONS OF ISRAEL, MOSES AND AARON FELL DOWN, FACE TO THE GROUND (14:5). JOSHUA . . . AND CALEB . . . TORE THEIR GARMENTS (14:6); AND THEY SAID TO THE ENTIRE COMMUNITY OF THE SONS OF ISRAEL (14:7), . . . "IF YAHWEH IS PLEASED WITH US, HE WILL LEAD US INTO THIS LAND AND GIVE IT TO US. IT IS A LAND WHERE MILK AND HONEY FLOW (14:8). DO NOT REBEL AGAINST YAHWEH. AND DO NOT BE AFRAID OF THE PEOPLE OF THIS LAND; WE SHALL GOBBLE THEM UP" (14:9). What great confidence in God. "Do not be afraid of them."

Do you know what the community did? They wanted to stone them. They wanted to stone Aaron, Moses, Caleb, and Joshua for no other reason except their tremendous confidence in God; and their confidence was based on proof—past performance. You know, it wasn't as if these people had not known God. Why do we do the same thing in our lives? Why is it we don't trust Him? Why is it that we always come up against something and we think, "Now, this is the time when God's hand will fall short? He will not provide for us this time." Why do we do that?

And if you wanted to know what God thought about this whole thing, He suddenly appeared in the Tent of Meeting AND YAHWEH SAID TO MOSES: "HOW LONG WILL THIS PEOPLE INSULT ME? HOW LONG WILL THEY REFUSE TO BELIEVE IN ME

DESPITE THE SIGNS I HAVE WORKED AMONG THEM? (14:11). I WILL STRIKE THEM WITH PESTILENCE AND DISOWN THEM. AND OF YOU I SHALL MAKE A NEW NATION, GREATER AND MIGHTIER THAN THEY ARE" (14:2).

Then comes Moses, that gentle, humble man, and he's diplomatic and very shrewd. You know, flattery will get you everywhere. I can't say it was flattery because that's an evil (it's insincere), but Moses was beautifully truthful and he brought to God's attention a point. I want you to listen to this. I think it's beautifully clever, and it is a perfect example of how to pray in the midst of great turmoil and darkness of soul, in the midst of an impossible situation.

This is his prayer: He says, "BUT THE EGYPTIANS ALREADY KNOW THAT YOU, BY YOUR OWN POWER, HAVE BROUGHT THIS PEOPLE OUT FROM THEIR MIDST (14:13). THEY HAVE SAID AS MUCH TO THE INHABITANTS OF THIS COUNTRY" (14:14). In other words, here's the Egyptians saying to the people before the Israelites ever arrive, "Watch out. These people have a great God who does wonders for them." "THEY ALREADY KNOW THAT YOU, YAHWEH, ARE IN THE MIDST OF THIS PEOPLE, AND THAT YOU SHOW YOURSELF TO THEM FACE TO FACE; THAT IT IS YOU, YAHWEH, WHOSE CLOUD STANDS OVER THEM, THAT YOU GO BEFORE THEM IN A PILLAR OF CLOUD BY DAY AND A PILLAR OF FIRE BY NIGHT (14:14). IF YOU DESTROY THIS PEOPLE NOW AS IF IT WERE ONE MAN, THEN THE NATIONS WHO HAVE HEARD ABOUT YOU WILL SAY (14:15), 'YAHWEH WAS NOT ABLE TO BRING THIS PEOPLE INTO THE LAND HE SWORE TO GIVE THEM'" (14:16). Ah-ha, isn't that clever? Then he adds: "IT IS NOW YOU WHO MUST DISPLAY YOUR POWER, ACCORDING TO THOSE WORDS YOU SPOKE" (14:17).

You know what he said here? Moses has just said that it takes greater omnipotence and greater power to forgive than to do great things. We don't often think of that, do we? When we think of offending God, whose nature is so far above our own, we don't always realize that it takes great power for God to be merciful. Did you ever want to swat your kid on the head for some dumb thing he did? Doesn't it take a lot more energy to restrain yourself than to let him have it? We must think about this, in this instance, because this is what Moses has said: "YAHWEH IS SLOW TO ANGER AND RICH IN GRACIOUSNESS, FORGIVING FAULTS AND TRANSGRESSION, AND YET LETTING NOTHING GO UNCHECKED" (14:18).

Later Yahweh says to them: "NOT ONE SHALL SEE THE LAND I SWORE TO GIVE THEIR FATHERS. NOT ONE OF THOSE WHO SLIGHT ME SHALL SEE IT. BUT (14:23) MY SERVANT CALEB IS OF ANOTHER SPIRIT. BECAUSE HE HAS OBEYED ME PERFECTLY, I WILL BRING HIM INTO THE LAND (14:24). . . . I WILL DEAL WITH YOU ACCORDING TO THE VERY WORDS YOU HAVE USED IN MY HEARING (14:28). IN THIS WILDERNESS YOUR DEAD BODIES WILL FALL, . . . ALL YOU WHO WERE NUMBERED FROM THE AGE OF TWENTY YEARS AND OVER, YOU WHO HAVE COMPLAINED AGAINST ME (14:29). I SWEAR THAT YOU SHALL NOT ENTER THE LAND. . . . IT IS CALEB . . . AND JOSHUA (14:30) . . . AND YOUR YOUNG CHILDREN THAT YOU SAID WOULD BE SEIZED AS BOOTY, IT IS THESE I SHALL BRING TO KNOW THE LAND YOU HAVE DISDAINED" (14:31).

It's just beautiful how the Lord hears every word you say. This was perfect justice because they had rebelled against Him. They had rejected Him. They had doubted His providence, His mercy and His love, and they were not deserving. But He is merciful. He took the very complaint they had and brought beautiful love out of it and beautiful mercy. The children they thought they would lose would be the only ones to inherit the land. This is simply beautiful.

Do you see what the Father wants? Trust. Don't ever say, "This is impossible." Don't ever say, "This can't be done." It may not be done in the way you want it, in the time you want, but it will be done. This is what you must understand. Once you give this problem or these children or these people to God, you must leave them to God in full trust.

Striking the Rock Ourselves

❖

Numbers 20:5–11

The Israelites say to Moses, "WHY DID YOU LEAD US OUT OF EGYPT, ONLY TO BRING US TO THIS WRETCHED PLACE? IT IS A PLACE UNFIT FOR SOWING, IT HAS NO FIGS, NO VINES, NO POMEGRANATES, AND THERE IS NOT EVEN WATER TO DRINK!" (20:5). These people were constantly aggravating poor Moses, and no matter what great wonders the Lord performed for them, they were always looking back on what they had lost. We all have a tendency to look back and to focus on our past lives or on the things that happened before. The past seems to be so much better than what's happening now. We edit out all of the bad stuff and only recall the happiness of the past—then we compare that to the misery of the present moment. Pretty soon we're recalling "the good old days." You look back in your life and you say, "Oh, when my husband and I were courting it was so beautiful." The first year you were married you looked forward to his coming home with great anticipation. Now you look up at the clock and when that little hand hits the six you think: "Here comes the monster. Well, he'll be gone by eight o'clock tomorrow. He's not the man I married." This is just something in our human nature, I think. The evil one perhaps puts these things in our minds in order to make us dissatisfied with God's will in the present moment. The important thing to remember is that you have the Lord who is eternally young, eternal happiness, eternal joy, eternal strength. And you have Him. Don't be grousing like the Israelites.

LEAVING THE ASSEMBLY, MOSES AND AARON WENT TO THE DOOR OF THE TENT OF MEETING. THEY THREW THEMSELVES FACE DOWNWARD ON THE GROUND (20:6). Did you ever pray that way? It's a very efficacious way to pray. And YAHWEH SPOKE TO MOSES AND SAID (20:7), "TAKE THE BRANCH AND CALL THE COMMUNITY TOGETHER, YOU AND YOUR BROTHER AARON. THEN, IN FULL VIEW OF THEM, ORDER THIS ROCK TO GIVE WATER. YOU WILL MAKE WATER FLOW FOR THEM OUT OF THE ROCK, AND PRO-VIDE DRINK FOR THE COMMUNITY AND THEIR CATTLE" (20:8). Now, you know, it would be very easy to draw water out of the ground, but to draw water out of a rock is something totally dif-ferent. Sometimes the Lord does that in your life. He lets you wait until you get down to the bare rock of your soul—until you feel nothing. There is no place to go, there is nothing to do, everything is dark and bare and absolutely hopeless. Then suddenly out of nowhere comes water: relief, hope, a new life. Sometimes the Lord permits everything we desire to turn into its opposite; the things we wanted turn to ashes. Why does He permit this? So that when I am relieved, when I am comforted, I will recognize that it is from God alone.

MOSES TOOK UP THE BRANCH FROM BEFORE YAHWEH, AS HE HAD DIRECTED HIM (20:9). THEN MOSES AND AARON CALLED THE ASSEMBLY TOGETHER IN FRONT OF THE ROCK AND ADDRESSED THEM, "LISTEN NOW, YOU REBELS" (20:10). Moses is finally getting impatient. "SHALL WE MAKE WATER GUSH FROM THIS ROCK FOR YOU?" (20:10). Question mark. AND MOSES RAISED HIS HAND AND STRUCK THE ROCK TWICE WITH THE BRANCH;

WATER GUSHED IN ABUNDANCE, AND THE COMMUNITY DRANK AND THEIR CATTLE TOO (20:11).

First of all he said, "YOU REBELS." Do you remember how meek and gentle he's been up till now? He's always interceding for these people, always praying for them. Now he's had it up to here. He says, "Shall we get water out of this rock, you rebels?" and he hits it twice. Ah, what's happened to Moses? He has looked at the difficulty—and that's all he saw. He has looked at the impossible situation, getting water out of a rock. He has looked at the meanness, the ingratitude, the impatience, the unkindness of this people and he's let it get to him. He's so angry that he doubts God. He thinks: "Shall we do this? I wonder if the water will come after all this. Maybe God's mercy has reached its limit." Moses's patience has reached its limit and he has judged God by himself. We are constantly doing the same. We are constantly judging God by ourselves. "I will not forgive, so God will not forgive. . . . I will love you if you do this, but if you do that, brother, that's it. That's it!"

So Moses reached a limit in his life; he got angry with these people. He didn't see a people wandering in the desert needing God; he saw only a stiff-necked, rebellious, selfish, ungrateful people. He let that situation come within, and once it got within, he doubted the mercy of God toward them. You see he *insulted* God, and we do this all the time. I say, "Lord, I believe in your providence but I worry about tomorrow." I say, "Lord, I believe your infinite wisdom has planned everything for me, but I still don't understand why things happen or their timing." I say, "God, I believe You have created all things." Then I wonder, "Did He create me, and if He did, why? I believe God that You have a plan for everything, and yet I doubt I exist for any reason."

Are we doing the same as Moses? I say, "Lord, I believe in Your healing powers." Yet I refuse to believe that the pain I have could be the healing for a sickness more serious than physical—the physical illness could well cure a more lethal spiritual malady that I am riddled with. We look at God and claim to believe in Him, but our actions and our thoughts don't correspond to our beliefs. Here's the difference between belief and faith: Belief is to know. Faith is to see.

God Uses the Weak

❖

Judges 6:10–16; 7:2–7

Look at Gideon in chapter six of the book of Judges. God again uses a very weak man (and a few others) to confound a strong army.

You might have heard the story of Teresa of Ávila who was riding in a carriage one day on her way to build a foundation. The carriage got stuck in the mud and the Lord appeared to her. She asked Him, "Why did You do this? You know I am in a hurry." And the Lord said, "This is how I treat my friends." Teresa replied, "No wonder You have so few of them." Gideon is saying the same thing here.

God says, "I AM YAHWEH YOUR GOD" (6:10). Then Gideon says, "FORGIVE ME, MY LORD, BUT IF YAHWEH IS WITH US, THEN WHY IS IT THAT ALL THIS IS HAPPENING TO US NOW?" (6:13). Finally Yahweh says, "GO IN THE STRENGTH NOW UPHOLDING YOU, AND YOU WILL RESCUE ISRAEL FROM THE POWER OF MIDIAN" (6:14). GIDEON ANSWERED HIM, "FORGIVE ME, MY LORD, BUT HOW CAN I DELIVER ISRAEL? MY CLAN, YOU MUST KNOW, IS THE

WEAKEST IN MANASSEH AND I AM THE LEAST IMPORTANT IN MY FAMILY" (6:15). He had the same idea we have today. You have to have a name to do anything, you have to be somebody, or you have to belong to a particular class of people. You need a degree with a couple of letters behind your name. Gideon had the same idea. YAHWEH ANSWERED HIM, "I WILL BE WITH YOU AND YOU SHALL CRUSH MIDIAN AS THOUGH IT WERE A SINGLE MAN" (6:16).

We know that Gideon got an army together. The Scripture tells us that YAHWEH SAID TO GIDEON, "THERE ARE TOO MANY PEOPLE WITH YOU FOR ME TO PUT MIDIAN INTO THEIR POWER; ISRAEL MIGHT CLAIM THE CREDIT FOR THEMSELVES AT MY EX-PENSE: THEY MIGHT SAY, 'MY OWN HAND HAS RESCUED ME' (7:2). THEREFORE, MAKE THIS PROCLAMATION NOW TO THE PEOPLE: 'LET ANYONE WHO IS FRIGHTENED OR FEARFUL GO HOME!'" . . . TWENTY-TWO THOUSAND MEN WENT HOME, AND TEN THOUSAND WERE LEFT (7:3). They looked at Gideon and said, "This man is going to deliver us?!"

Today we have forgotten that for all the technology and intelligence in the world, it is still God Who does everything. God went so far as to have Gideon take all his remaining men to the waterside and observe how they drank. If they drank like a dog, lapping with their tongue, the Lord put them aside. These were the three hundred imbeciles God chose to save Israel. Gideon ended up with three hundred stupid idiots (Jgs 7:4–7). And as Gideon began to see his army dwindle from ten thousand to three hundred he got a little scared, and he thought, "Maybe I am not hearing God. What's the whole pur-pose behind this?"

Today we are fighting tremendous invisible armies. Armies who are more intelligent than we are—evil spirits. We are weak, we are oppressed on every side by the flesh, the world, and the devil: the three great tempters. Gideon was strong with the strength of God. God wants to tell the whole world: I am going to do it. The weaker we are, the more confidence we should have. God uses the weak things of this world to confound the strong. Whether you are a child, an old person, or a sick person, if you love Jesus, you can be a terror to the invisible foe.

God Wins the Battle

❖

Judges 7:12–22

When Gideon's enemies, the Midianites, descended on their camels THE VALLEY [WAS] AS THICK AS LOCUSTS (7:12). That's how many men there were. THEIR CAMELS WERE INNUMERABLE LIKE THE SAND ON THE SEASHORE (7:12). I want you to visualize in your imagination this throng of people and poor Gideon standing there with only three hundred uncouth, uncultured men. GIDEON CAME UP JUST AS A MAN WAS TELLING HIS COMRADE A DREAM [HE HAD HAD] (7:13). The Lord was trying so hard to encourage Gideon. The Midianite said: "I HAD A DREAM: A CAKE MADE OF BARLEY BREAD CAME ROLLING THROUGH THE CAMP OF MIDIAN; IT REACHED THE TENT, STRUCK AGAINST IT AND TURNED IT UPSIDE DOWN" (7:13). HIS COMRADE ANSWERED, "THIS CAN BE NOTHING ELSE THAN THE SWORD OF GIDEON. . . . GOD HAS PUT MIDIAN AND ALL THE CAMP INTO HIS POWER" (7:14).

What happened? Psychological warfare. The Lord had allowed the Midianites to have such a fear of Gideon. The poor guy hadn't even done anything yet, not one thing. Now, you're talking about a throng of people so large that they couldn't even be counted. Probably 300,000 people.

WHEN GIDEON HEARD THE DREAM . . . HE FELL TO HIS KNEES; THEN HE RETURNED TO THE CAMP OF ISRAEL AND SAID, "ON YOUR FEET, FOR YAHWEH HAS PUT THE CAMP OF MIDIAN INTO YOUR POWER!" (7:15). There, now he's brave. Oh, boy, is he brave. GIDEON THEN DIVIDED HIS THREE HUNDRED MEN INTO THREE COMPANIES (7:16). This is one of the most unbelievable battles. To each man he gave what? An arrow? A bow? A sword? Nope. He gave each of them an empty pitcher with a torch inside, and a horn. He lights the torch, hides it under a pitcher, and holds onto the horn.

Gideon says, "WATCH ME, AND DO AS I DO. WHEN I REACH THE EDGE OF THE CAMP, WHATEVER I DO, YOU DO TOO" (7:17). Now you know those three hundred men had to have a certain level of stupidity. Absolute stupidity, because they've already seen the Midianites in the valley, like locusts, and here they are like people going to a New Year's Eve party. Just imagine these men walking in the dark, hiding a torch, and a horn. A horn!

Scripture says, GIDEON AND HIS HUNDRED COMPANIONS REACHED THE EDGE OF THE CAMP AT THE BEGINNING OF THE MIDDLE WATCH, WHEN THE NEW SENTRIES HAD JUST BEEN POSTED; THEY SOUNDED THEIR HORNS AND SMASHED THE PITCHERS IN THEIR HANDS (7:19). Toot-do-la-loooo. Smash! THE THREE COMPANIES SOUNDED THEIR HORNS AND SMASHED THEIR PITCHERS; WITH THEIR LEFT HANDS THEY GRASPED THE TORCHES, WITH THEIR RIGHT HANDS THE HORNS READY TO BLOW (7:20). What a way to win a battle. AND THEY SHOUTED, "FOR YAHWEH AND (FOR) GIDEON!" (7:20). AND THEY STOOD STILL. . . . THEN

THE WHOLE CAMP WOKE UP AND THE MIDIANITES FLED, SHOUTING (7:21). WHILE THE THREE HUNDRED KEPT SOUNDING THEIR HORNS, YAHWEH MADE EVERY MAN IN THE CAMP TURN HIS SWORD AGAINST HIS COMRADE (7:22). That was it. See, they thought they were fighting Gideon! It was dark and they saw these three hundred torches, which must have looked like thousands of people coming down into the valley, and they all fled. Gideon's army never moved a step.

Lord, we pray that we can be your Gideons today. Where they stood on a mountain with a horn and a covered torch, we stand before the Blessed Sacrament with the horn of confidence and the torch of our love, and we stand still. We stand still. We don't turn to the right or to the left—shaky knees and all—we stand still. That is our own method of fighting a massive battle. God has to win every battle for us.

So today in our interior lives let's be like Gideon. God calls us to great holiness. God calls us to help save His people and return them to their Father's house. We must be willing in all our weakness, in all our infidelities, in our lack of virtue, to let the Lord use us as He did Gideon. We have only to stand still with our torches, with our love, and pray. That's it. God Himself will destroy the locusts of this age; those who are eating up the fruits of the Lord, those who have forgotten that it is God Almighty who is victorious, no one else.

Ruth and Obedience

❖

Ruth 1:1–22

*A*t an investment ceremony for one of her nuns, Sister Ruth
*Marie, Mother Angelica offered this off-the-cuff meditation
on the Old Testament heroine Ruth.*

As you know from reading the Scriptures, the name of
Ruth is very important. She left the land when the Moabites
were getting after the Israelites. She was a Moabite. She could
have gone home. Moabites were not very loved by the Israelites—they were kind of pagan. Her mother-in-law, Naomi
(who had one other daughter-in-law) said to Ruth, "You go
back to your people now." Ruth said, "No, no. I'm not leaving
you. Your people will be my people. Your God, my God." The
essence of Ruth is a willingness to follow in darkness.

She didn't know anything about the real, true God. But
she had what it took to believe in the One True God! She's
kind of the grandma of Jesus. Ruth was a strong woman. Ready
for anything, and God rewarded her for her obedience and her
love.

If there's one thing people who want to follow the Lord
need today, it is to have no fear, no excuses, and no concern for
human respect. Loyalty was Ruth's great gift from God. She
remained with her mother-in-law—and it was the love for her
mother-in-law that sustained her. She was loyal, and because
she was loyal, she was obedient. That's something we never
think about. Disobedience is a crime against loyalty. Ruth was

the epitome of obedience in the Old Testament. In a new land, among new people, she was always obedient.

Some of us think we have to like what we're doing to be obedient. You're not being obedient until you do what you don't like to do. If you don't believe me, ask Ruth.

Saul and the Will of God

❖

1 Samuel 15:17–21

Like Saul we often think that what we want to give God is better than what God asks of us. That's why Saul was punished. The whole kingdom was taken away from him. He exercised a lot of self-will, which came from his pride. Saul forgot to give God credit, and only obeyed God halfway.

In his mind Saul thought: "Well, I'll take the best livestock and I'll sacrifice those." But that isn't what the Lord asked! The Lord said, "Do away with everything, and don't save anybody." But Saul saved the king. That's called disobedience, and the Lord was angry. There's nothing that angers the Lord like disobedience. Nothing. It's one of the traps Saul fell into (we all do from time to time). He felt his idea was better than the Lord's. His idea was "I'll give the animals I spare to the Lord." And the Lord said, "[O]BEDIENCE IS BETTER THAN SACRIFICE" (15:22).

See, you can't use your own human reason when you're talking about God's will. You can't add to His will or detract from it. Just do what He is asking of you. Saul used his head and lost the kingdom, lost the inspiration of God—and when that happens everything else rushes in: concupiscence and jealousy and all the rest.

Now, we with our modern minds think, well, gee, it doesn't look too bad. He did sacrifice to God what he kept (and then he kept the king). But that was total disobedience. You may want to do something novel and it may seem better to you, but is it better in the eyes of God? Saul thought he was enhancing the Lord's will. But it wasn't pleasing to God, and if you do that in your daily life, you can knock yourself right out of the box because that's the way God is.

He cares about obedience to His will. We see it most dramatically in the nakedness of death. When you die, you don't take anything with you. What would you use it for anyway? Are you going to give Saint Peter a $10 tip for getting you in the gate? At that point it is all about how obedient you were to the will of God. Are you using reasoning to be disobedient? It doesn't work. It didn't work for Saul. And it is not going to work for you.

Saul's reasoning was "Look, I have all these nice fat calves. God would like these." Then he tries to get clever. He even said, "I did what the Lord told me to do. I killed all the men, all the children. I took the animals for sacrifice, which I gave to the Lord." Now, that looks very reasonable. He kept the king, which he didn't mention. But he did not do God's will and the Lord just knocked him out. Saul did a typical human thing: He reasoned himself out of obedience. Do not follow his error.

David and the Love of God

❖

1 Samuel 17:22–51

The battle between Goliath and David is instructional. It's reasonable that a rock, be it ever so small, thrust at the right speed, could embed itself into your head, especially if it was guided by God Himself. What amazes me about that incident is that everybody, including King Saul, was so petrified that they allowed this kid to face Goliath. They probably thought they had lost the battle. They weren't even embarrassed to send this young man over there. It shows how scared they were and apparently paralyzed—all the generals, the soldiers, everyone was paralyzed.

This Goliath could have very well been eight, nine feet tall, and nobody was going to take him on. It shows how our souls become paralyzed by the appearance of an obstacle—and that's when we make wrong decisions. See, King Saul already knew he was not blessed by God—that God was very displeased with him, and the way he executed his office. His mission had been taken away from him. But let's not get so spiritually paralyzed by our own faults, the faults of others, by circumstances, by work, by our health, by the events in the world, that we lose sight of the most important thing: the call of God.

The thing to remember about David is he was really a sinner and yet Our Lord loved him so much that He's known as the Son of David. David did some pretty bad things: he shed a lot of blood, he was cruel in battle, he had that thing going with Bathsheba and then he murdered her husband. David should be an encouragement to any of you who might get discouraged over your little peccadilloes. Once the Lord loves you, I tell you, it's unbelievable. His love is forever.

Elijah and the Still, Small Voice

❖

1 Kings 19:5–14

It's so easy to be holy. So easy to give our total self to the Lord, in total abandonment to His Love and to His will. What a wonderful goal. What a mission. We're often sent into the wilderness *of ourselves* to seek the true light. That's where we're all sent: into the wilderness of ourselves. . . . We're sent by God on that journey of the soul, sent into the interior wilderness to find the One Who sent us there. That's why I like the prophet Elijah so much.

I'm so glad he's going to come back. I hope I'm around when he does. I've always pictured him as a small, scrawny little guy with a long beard and a squeaky voice, aggravating everybody all the time. Getting real discouraged and saying, "Lord take me, I'm no better than my fathers." An angel wakes Elijah up at one point. He looks at the angel, and he's not impressed. The angel gives him a cake, he eats it, and falls back to sleep: that is depression. Depression! The angel wakes him up again, "Eat. You've got to go to Mount Horeb." Hmm. He gets up, eats, and he walks for forty days and forty nights. Can you imagine walking without ceasing for forty days and forty nights—no sleep, no food, just walking?

He gets all the way to the top of Mount Horeb and here comes an earthquake. He watched and looked for God, but

God was not in the earthquake. Then there was a fire on the mountain—big fire—and God was not in the fire. Then there was such thunder and lightning that the whole mountain shook, and there was no voice of God at all. Elijah is standing there wondering, "Why am I here? I'm soaking wet, it's cold. I've gone through an earthquake, a fire, and a storm." Then comes the most beautiful passage: [T]HERE CAME THE SOUND OF A GENTLE BREEZE (19:12). And he took his mantle and hid his face with it. You know what I think the fire and the storm and the earthquake were? His soul. His soul, his wilderness was like an earthquake, fiery and storm-tossed. God had to manifest to Elijah exteriorly what he was interiorly.

Remember Elijah had killed all of Baal's prophets. Jezebel was after him and she said, "May I be cursed if by tomorrow morning you're not as one of these prophets"—the ones Elijah chopped up. So he runs. What else can he do? He's discouraged, he's disgruntled, he's unhappy, and I think that was a reflection of the inside of Elijah. Only when he came to a deep awareness that "there's something wrong with me," only then did he hear that gentle voice, that still, small voice of God. And he covered his face and he said . . . nothing. He was absolutely silent. The next sentence is so perfect that only God could have come up with it. He said, "Elijah, what are you doing here?" and Elijah said, "I have fled. There's not anybody left but me, and I know better than the rest of them. Jezebel is after me because I killed all the prophets. And I'm tired of this being a prophet. I'm tired of the whole thing. I want out." The Lord said, "Elijah, go back where you were." Another forty days and forty nights' walk. Only there was no little angelic biscuit this time. . . . God tells him, "There are others who have also been faithful. Now go back and do your duty as a prophet of the Lord." Just imagine what that poor guy's soul had to go through before he could hear the whisper of God.

Like Elijah, we will only hear God's voice when we allow our wilderness to be calm and quiet. As long as your wilderness is consumed by storms, earthquakes, or fires, you can't hear His voice. You can't hear His voice—and you need to.

God Is Watching

❖

Psalm 139

If you are ever in a kind of tragic situation and you don't know what to do, and your mind just goes blank, I would go to the Psalms. Look at a Psalm that I like very much. It's Psalm 139 and it praises the omnipotence of God. It starts like this: YAHWEH, YOU EXAMINE ME AND KNOW ME, YOU KNOW IF I AM STANDING OR SITTING, YOU READ MY THOUGHTS FROM FAR AWAY (1–2). Now, can you imagine that? You don't pay attention to anybody whether they're standing or sitting, you're just happy if they're quiet. But He knows your every move. "You examine me, and know me." Some of you don't think God knows you. Sweetheart, you're no surprise to God. He decided you would be before time began.

I love that line: YOU READ MY THOUGHTS FROM FAR AWAY. You know the Lord did just that. When Jesus called Nathaniel to be one of the apostles, He said to the others, "Here's a man without guile." And Nathaniel heard Him and said, "How do You know me?" Jesus looked at him and said, "When you were under the fig tree, I saw you." Just think about that. When you walked in and picked up this book, and sat down on your sofa or laid in your bed, God knew you did it, and He saw you do it. I mean, that's the kind of attention you get from God. All the sin that you commit in the dark—you are not hiding it from anybody, especially from God. You can rob a bank in the dead of night, but it's bright as the noonday sun to Him.

It says here: [W]HETHER I WALK OR LIE DOWN, YOU ARE WATCHING, YOU KNOW EVERY DETAIL OF MY CONDUCT (3). There are no secrets hidden from God. You know, sometimes you come home from work and you're tired and you think, "Well, I'll just lie down on the sofa for a few minutes and rest." He sees you, He knows you, and He loves you. We don't have that kind of love, do we? We don't have the kind of love that envelops everything a person does whether it be good or bad or sorrowful—but God loves us at every moment.

It says here: THE WORD IS NOT EVEN ON MY TONGUE, YAH-WEH, BEFORE YOU KNOW ALL ABOUT IT; CLOSE BEHIND AND CLOSE IN FRONT YOU FENCE ME ROUND, SHIELDING ME WITH YOUR HAND (4–5). If we knew this one little truth about God, we'd never be lonely again. Many times God shields you with His hand and you don't even know it. We need to thank God for those times. We need to thank God for all the things He does for us without our knowledge!

I remember one time after my spinal operation many years ago, I was driving with this woman to receive some follow-up treatments, and she was talking and talking. She was about to turn in to the hospital and all of a sudden in front of me, on the passenger side, was the approaching radiator of a big bus. I could feel the heat because this woman didn't look to her side as she started to turn. Had that bus driver not turned onto the sidewalk, I would have been killed. We probably would have both been killed. But you see, God shielded us with His hand there. This happens to all of you at various points in your lives.

The Psalmist continues: SUCH KNOWLEDGE IS BEYOND MY UNDERSTANDING, A HEIGHT TO WHICH MY MIND CANNOT ATTAIN (6). I love this Psalm. WHERE COULD I GO TO ESCAPE YOUR SPIRIT? WHERE COULD I FLEE FROM YOUR PRESENCE? (7). You know, often in our spiritual lives we act as if God is not present. So many of you feel abandoned, alone—you think God is not there. When you feel dry, you think God is not there. When you can't pray, you think God is not there. How easily we forget about this one sentence: WHERE COULD I FLEE FROM YOUR PRESENCE? (7). IF I CLIMB THE HEAVENS, YOU ARE THERE, THERE TOO, IF I LIE IN SHEOL (8). IF I FLEW TO THE POINT OF SUNRISE, OR WESTWARD ACROSS THE SEA (9), YOUR HAND WOULD STILL BE GUIDING ME, YOUR RIGHT HAND HOLDING ME (10). There's just no way and nowhere you can go without God going with you. You can be devastated in weakness, and yet His strength is there. His presence is there. It is an awesome reality.

Isn't it wonderful to have somebody who loves you that much, always. And He's not going on vacation! He's not going to leave you! He's never going to let you down! He's always there. You know, when I was a young Sister, I was kind of ornery. Well, I still am, I guess. Reverend Mother was teaching us how to meditate, and she said, "You place yourself in the presence of God." I would think to myself, "Well, that's not so hard. I can't get out of His presence. He's everywhere." (The smart novice suddenly enters the order and knows everything.) I was stupid. . . . But it's true! Where can you go to escape His presence? Even though you may be alone and even though people abandon you and your children don't pay attention to you, you have God. You have God! And He has always been there.

A little further down the Psalm reads: YOU KNOW ME THROUGH AND THROUGH (14), FROM HAVING WATCHED MY BONES TAKE SHAPE WHEN I WAS BEING FORMED IN SECRET, KNITTED TOGETHER IN THE LIMBO OF THE WOMB (15). Isn't that awesome? God is there at your first moment. Without God nothing living would exist. If God were to stop thinking of me at this moment, you would see a great big grease spot and a habit on this chair.

Let's go to the end of Psalm 139; it's a prayer really. Pray this whenever you can: GOD, EXAMINE ME AND KNOW MY HEART, PROBE ME AND KNOW MY THOUGHTS (23); MAKE SURE I DO NOT FOLLOW PERNICIOUS WAYS, AND GUIDE ME IN THE WAY THAT IS EVERLASTING (24). Amen. Seek His presence and listen for His call. He is there.

DON'T BE A WHAT'S-NEXTER

There's always a grave temptation, very subtle at times, to say: "I've heard it all. What's next?" Well, if you say that, it means you don't know a thing.

Saint Francis used to spend a whole night, a whole night, in prayer and he'd say nothing but "My Lord and my God." That's all he said all night long, and then he'd think about it. Now, in our brilliant minds we'd say, "Yeah, okay. My Lord and my God. I know that. What's next?"

You see, when you become a what's-nexter, then pride—and that's what it is—pride will destroy you because you close your mind to grace, to the grace and the power of the Spirit to give you more light on the same line of Scripture. Nobody can plumb the depths of one passage of Scripture—not if you spent your whole life. How many times have you heard the Scripture? I've been in religious life forty-three years this year and so I've heard every part of Scripture—heard the Gospel preached more than forty times, not counting my earlier life. Assuming that you've heard it before and you already know it, what in the world would you ever learn from this Book? Why read it every day when you've already read it? It isn't going to change. It isn't like you get a revised edition every year with new information and new revelations.

Well, you can't treat the inner self and this Book as if you're cramming for finals, because if we don't meditate on what we already know, we don't grow. If we don't let the Spirit open up new vistas and new light and new grace, what a great gift we are missing. You wouldn't have to learn a darn thing more if you were to meditate on God's Word and just allow it to come into your soul. We're talking about grace; we're not talking about knowledge. If you want knowledge, go get a degree. You can learn a lot. You can learn Scripture, but you may never *know it!*

We don't open ourselves to the light and grace of the Spirit because pride shuts the door. Pride says, "I've already heard that," and shuts out His Word in the Present Moment—in this new reality. I'm here to *experience* God. I'm here to have the kind of faith that brings Him into my life every day, every moment. I'm here to know God. I'm here to love God. You've got to get your mind out of the knowledge stage and into the experience stage.

God's Constancy

❖

Jeremiah 31:3; Isaiah 46:4

In Jeremiah it says "I HAVE LOVED YOU WITH AN EVERLASTING LOVE, SO I AM CONSTANT IN MY AFFECTION FOR YOU" (31:3). The Lord does not appeal to our animal nature. He appeals to our spiritual nature. He's trying to make us live now as we will in heaven.

He loved you from your mother's womb, before you were created (Psalm 139:13,15). God's eternal memory fascinates me. He wants to assure us that it doesn't change, that His affection is constant. He says in Isaiah 46:4: "IN YOUR OLD AGE I SHALL BE STILL THE SAME, WHEN YOUR HAIR IS GREY I SHALL STILL SUPPORT YOU. I HAVE ALREADY DONE SO, I HAVE CARRIED YOU, I SHALL STILL SUPPORT AND DELIVER YOU."

Our love varies and our affection is not constant, so we automatically attribute our puniness to God. But it just isn't so. I heard the mother of a pretty ornery kid say: "I look at him sometimes and I just can't imagine that he's still the same little, sweet, cute baby I used to hug. To think that this monster is the same child!" Our Lord is saying that He began with us and He will end with us. That's what it means to be constant. What a grace we have in God's constancy.

The New Testament

The Birth of Christ
(A Meditation)

❖

Luke 2:4–14

*I*n the 1970s Mother conducted a Bible study in the parlor of
her monastery for an ecumenical group of women for nearly
five years. She called the teachings "Journeys into Scripture."
Many of these were recorded for distribution and for broadcast on
a local radio station in Birmingham. The following meditation,
and subsequent ones, are excerpted from Mother's "Journeys."

On our spiritual journey we are going to Bethlehem and
we see Joseph and Mary looking for a room. Joseph is quite
confident that he will find a place for the night. So he goes
to the best inn in Bethlehem, and they say, "There is no room
here. Can't you see we're overcrowded?" So he goes to another
inn and there is no vacancy there. They go to the house of relatives and there is no room there either. He goes to Mary and
she smiles, she understands.

They make their way toward the gate of the city. Joseph
spies a cave there and he looks at Mary. She nods. He lays
his cloak out and puts some fresh hay in the corner and he
asks Mary to sit down. Then he goes to the mouth of the cave
and lights a fire and sits down. As I look at the scene I think,
How strange this is. So many people waited for centuries for
this night and when it comes, there is no one here. Suddenly
the whole cave is filled with the most brilliant light: beautiful
and soft. At the end of the cave is Mary. She is kneeling and

she has the most lovely Infant in her arms. My heart begins to pound with joy and I go over and kneel, and I say to her, "May I touch him?" She says, "Yes. Don't be afraid. This is why He came so that you would see your God in the flesh and never be afraid again." I go to grasp His hand and instead He clasps my little finger and holds it so tight. I realize how much God loves me—that He would come in such a tiny form to such a cold, simple place. That He would consent to be so dependent on His creatures: Mary and Joseph to give Him food and drink and to care for Him. This God who created the whole universe is dependent upon two creatures, all out of love for me.

When I go out of the cave it is so dark. There is no one in sight. I see a great light in the sky and hear angels' voices. Perhaps now people will come? But only a few shepherds appear: the simple, the lowly, the humble; those whose hearts were made ready for His coming by poverty and suffering. They heard the angels. We go in together and we kneel down before the Child and He looks at us and smiles—a smile of such love as if to say, "I came for you." I say: "Oh God, give me the humility to give love for love—that as You came for me, so I may live for Thee. In my heart may You always find shelter and a warm inn where You may dwell, as in a temple, in splendor and glory. At every moment I wish to say I love Thee my God, I love Thee." Mary and Joseph look at me happily. They determined long ago that God would always find a place in their hearts.

Following the Star

❖

Matthew 2:9–11

Let's take up the second chapter, ninth verse of Saint Matthew's Gospel, where he speaks of the wise men. HAVING LISTENED TO WHAT THE KING HAD TO SAY, THEY SET OUT. AND THERE IN FRONT OF THEM WAS THE STAR THEY HAD SEEN RISING; IT WENT FORWARD AND HALTED OVER THE PLACE WHERE THE CHILD WAS (2:9). THE SIGHT OF THE STAR FILLED THEM WITH DELIGHT (2:10). It is amazing that no one else seemed to see the star. Which is a kind of lesson for us, because obviously that star was very big, very bright, and moving—so much so that they could follow it. Isn't it strange that they were the only ones who saw it? You would think that a phenomenon of that proportion would be seen by everybody.

It makes you wonder if maybe there are stars in our lives that we don't see for whatever reason. If there aren't great graces that God has in store, moving in front of us, but because we're so caught up in things—people, events, work, health, whatever—we don't see them. We don't see the stars; we don't see the opportunities. Every opportunity for virtue is a moving star. The very fact that it passes so quickly indicates that it moves. These are stars in your crown, a gift from heaven created by God just for you. So I think we need to be careful that we're not like the people of the city of Bethlehem or Jerusalem.

I think we need to just ponder this. You know, that's one of the things Our Lady did, at least twice, according to Scripture. When the shepherds told her what the angels said about her

Son, she "pondered" it in her heart (Lk 2:19). At the finding of the Child Jesus, she STORED UP (all she had seen) "IN HER HEART" (Lk 2:51). You've got to ponder what this means. What does God really want you to do? There are times when the star is moving and you have no time to ponder.

The will of God is manifested in the present moment; it's a moving star, and sometimes you've only got a few seconds to follow it. And if you follow it, it will always be a bit ahead of you. Then there are times it disappears, totally. It comes and it goes. The Lord has something definite in mind, just as He had something definite in mind for the wise men.

The Gift of the Magi
(A Meditation)

❖

Matthew 2:1–12

We see a caravan outside of Jerusalem after the birth of Christ. There are three kings called wise men. You can see they are very wealthy. Yet each of them has a beautiful humility. They ask some of the citizens of the town: "Can you tell us where the infant King is?" The people are puzzled. "We have no king but Herod," they say. Have the wise men been mistaken? Was the star a figment of their imaginations? No, they are certain that this is the time for the birth of the great King. So they go to the king of the Jews, the great Herod. They ask him to lead them to the infant King. When you look at Herod, you see only hatred and jealousy. There will be no rival—no king but Herod. He calls the chief priests and the scribes and he demands to know what this is all about. They say, "This is the time when God was to send the Messiah, and He is to be born in Bethlehem."

We see Herod stroke his beard. He has a plan. He returns to the wise men and tells them to go on to Bethlehem and when they find Him, they are to report back to Herod so that he might also worship the Child. The wise men leave and they are once again led by this miraculous light that takes them to a house where they find Jesus, Mary, and Joseph. They kneel down and worship the infant King.

How odd it is: When He was born, Joseph and Mary saw only poor illiterate shepherds, now there are wise, wealthy, gentile kings. God is for all men, for all people, even as an infant, He came to save us all, and He would have homage and worship from all who are humble of heart. For those who seek Him no matter the obstacles, for those who are not ashamed to ask, "Where is the King?" for those who believe when they discover Him, He always reveals Himself.

What faith it takes to kneel down before this Infant and adore God so small. But these were truly wise men, who forgot their greatness before the majesty of God's Son: so humble, so tiny. Mary and Joseph are humbled that these great men would come to their home. I see in all of this not only love, but a great lesson. It is possible to be great and do great things and still be humble. It is possible to be poor and have nothing and to still be humble. It is possible to find our greatest treasure in God by being willing to give up the greatest things in the world. It is necessary to give up everything in me that is not Christlike and childlike. Oh Father, make me like Thine Son: small in the estimation of the world, but great in Thine eyes.

The Holy Innocents
(A Meditation)
❖

Matthew 2:13–18

The Scripture says: HEROD WAS FURIOUS WHEN HE REALISED THAT HE HAD BEEN OUTWITTED BY THE WISE MEN (2:16). We are at the palace of Herod in Jerusalem. Suddenly the chief priest comes in and says, "We have heard news that a king has been born in Bethlehem. Some say angels appeared and foretold this." Herod calls the palace guards and orders them to kill any male child two years or younger. Oh the evil of this man. Imagine this: He thinks he can destroy God's Son. Can it be that pride has reached its height?

What of God's Son? We go to Bethlehem and we see Jesus and Mary and Joseph and the wise men. They are all asleep. An angel of the Lord appears to the wise men in their sleep and he says, "Make haste, Herod wants to kill the Child. Do not go back to him. Return home another way." And the angel says to Joseph, "GET UP, TAKE THE CHILD AND HIS MOTHER WITH YOU, AND ESCAPE INTO EGYPT" (2:13). They rise and prepare the best they can, and each leaves by a different route.

Then I hear the soldiers coming. They are stomping through the streets and knocking on the doors. Any child two years and younger, they kill. Weeping and lamenting are heard all around, and I think, Why do these innocent children suffer for the greed and the ambition and the evil and the hatred of one man? For Herod? Why does God permit these children to die? Could He not have destroyed Herod? I look at the scene and I face a mystery, the mystery of life itself: evil, heartache, poverty, sickness. Why? And I realize that these children have had the privilege of dying for their God before their God died for them. God sent His Son to die for us. These children were given the privilege of being Christianity's first martyrs. Their mothers must have wondered and lamented. But as we look back we can see the good that came from this evil.

The glory of these children in heaven is incomprehensible because they were martyred for God's Son. So God permitted evil to bring about a greater good. Because they died, He lived. Because He died, WE live. It is a mystery that unless the seed falls to the ground and unless it dies, it remains alone. I realize that there are many things in me that must die before He can live: my pride, my ambition, my impatience, my anger. The difficulty I find in loving my neighbor, or listening to the problems of another. There is much that I must die to. But unless I die, unless these things are conquered, He cannot live in me. He cannot. For God must reign supreme in my soul. He must have all of me. He must know that I prefer Him to everyone and everything. I remember something He said on another day: I must take up my cross and follow Him—then like these Holy Innocents, I will have glory forever.

The Flight to Egypt

❖

Matthew 2:13–15

AFTER THEY HAD LEFT, THE ANGEL OF THE LORD APPEARED
TO JOSEPH IN A DREAM AND SAID, "GET UP, TAKE THE CHILD
AND HIS MOTHER WITH YOU, AND ESCAPE INTO EGYPT, AND STAY
THERE UNTIL I TELL YOU, BECAUSE HEROD INTENDS TO SEARCH
FOR THE CHILD AND DO AWAY WITH HIM" (2:13). SO JOSEPH GOT
UP AND, TAKING THE CHILD AND HIS MOTHER WITH HIM, LEFT
THAT NIGHT FOR EGYPT (2:14), WHERE HE STAYED UNTIL HEROD
WAS DEAD. THIS WAS TO FULFILL WHAT THE LORD HAD SPOKEN
THROUGH THE PROPHET: I CALLED MY SON OUT OF EGYPT (2:15).

God does things so differently from the way we would.
That's why we miss the boat many times—because we don't
think like God. You can't imagine the virtue of Saint Joseph,
because here he is, faced with a dream and off he goes.

It's strange that Herod wanted every child murdered two
years old and under. Now we don't know how much time
elapsed between the birth of Jesus and Herod's decree. What
we do know is that Joseph had all the responsibility of protect-
ing the Lord and Mary. Can you imagine that? We have to feel
the weight of the responsibility God has given to each of us
for our own souls and for the souls around us. You could say,
"Well, I don't know what my mission is." No one wrote Joseph
a detailed description of his mission either. He knew only one
thing at a time. He knew he had to take care of Mary and
Jesus, and that's all he knew.

Now, he's sent to a foreign country, full of idols. What

does he do? He had umpteen opportunities to practice faith. Having Mary and Jesus there didn't make it any easier on him. He didn't say, "Wait a minute, angel, you're telling me to go into Egypt tonight. Where?" He didn't ask the angel: "Where will we live?" or "How long will we stay?"

You see, we don't understand Joseph. We don't want uncertainty in our lives. You talk about uncertainty . . . the temptation certainly would have been for Joseph to say, "Look, I'm told this is the Son of God. This is the Messiah. Why should we be running to Egypt?" Our Lady had to give him faith and courage. But, you see, they didn't question God. When they heard "go," they went. Joseph could only do that if he was a great man of faith. And he was.

The Trust of the Holy Family (A Meditation)

❖

Matthew 2:13–15, 19–23

During our "Journey into Scripture" we are going to Bethlehem to a small house. The wise men have gone. Jesus, Mary, and Joseph are preparing for a journey. Their few belongings are placed on the back of a donkey and they go.

They begin their long trek into Egypt. The night is cold, and Joseph removes his cloak and places it around Mary and the Child. I can see Joseph looking a little anxious, worried perhaps. They stop beside a big palm tree. Mary and the Child rest beneath the branches of this beautiful tree, and Joseph sits beside them and looks out into the cold desert. As they sleep he wonders, Will they accept him, a stranger, a Jew in Egypt? Will he find work? Will there be a synagogue where they can worship the Child's father? Will they make friends? How long will they stay, and how will he know when to return?

I realize that he had the same problems that I have had many times: doubts and fears about the future, the hesitancy and the distrust of the present. The "whys" in my life are a mystery that I can only look at with trust—I must trust the Father, trust His love, and trust His will. As I look at the scene, I know what comes after. I can see God's will in this, but Joseph and Mary cannot. So I must learn a beautiful and very necessary lesson: During the times in my life when everything seems so dark and uncertain, I too must trust. I must believe that this is happening to me out of love: God's love, that somewhere in it there is good, my good. We see the Holy Family rise in the morning and begin their journey, and they go into Egypt. It is difficult, difficult to find work and to make friends, but in time they do.

Then another night comes, and during sleep, once more, Joseph is told he must return. He is told that the one who wanted to kill the Child is dead. What a mystery it is that God's Son waited until the danger was over, just as I must wait for many dangers to pass. Like Jesus and Joseph and Mary, I too must wait for God's will to unfold in my life. I too must pray and wait and love and hope—and never lose faith in the providence and love of my Father. So we see the Holy Family and we are not sure how old the Child was, perhaps He was five or six or eight. You can see them going back to Nazareth. On the way back Joseph wonders, Will he find his home in tatters? And what will his friends say when he returns?

They go back to Nazareth to begin a new life. I realize as I look at this scene that they needed deep faith and hope and love, and that I too, no matter what happens, must have faith and hope and love and great joy to do whatever my Father asks of me, because He loves me, and you.

The Disappearance of Jesus

❖

Luke 2:41–51

Let's look at that moment in Scripture when Jesus left the Holy Family. EVERY YEAR HIS PARENTS USED TO GO TO JE-RUSALEM FOR THE FEAST OF THE PASSOVER (2:41). WHEN HE WAS TWELVE YEARS OLD, THEY WENT UP FOR THE FEAST AS USUAL (2:42). WHEN THEY WERE ON THEIR WAY HOME AFTER THE FEAST, THE BOY JESUS STAYED BEHIND IN JERUSALEM WITHOUT HIS PAR-ENTS KNOWING IT (2:43). THEY ASSUMED HE WAS WITH THE CAR-AVAN, AND IT WAS ONLY AFTER A DAY'S JOURNEY THAT THEY WENT TO LOOK FOR HIM AMONG THEIR RELATIONS AND ACQUAINTANCES (2:44). WHEN THEY FAILED TO FIND HIM THEY WENT BACK TO JERUSALEM LOOKING FOR HIM EVERYWHERE (2:45). THREE DAYS LATER, THEY FOUND HIM IN THE TEMPLE, SITTING AMONG THE DOCTORS, LISTENING TO THEM, AND ASKING THEM QUESTIONS (2:46); AND ALL THOSE WHO HEARD HIM WERE ASTOUNDED AT HIS INTELLIGENCE AND HIS REPLIES (2:47). THEY WERE OVERCOME WHEN THEY SAW HIM, AND HIS MOTHER SAID TO HIM, "MY CHILD, WHY HAVE YOU DONE THIS TO US? SEE HOW WORRIED YOUR FA-THER AND I HAVE BEEN, LOOKING FOR YOU" (2:48). "WHY WERE YOU LOOKING FOR ME?" HE REPLIED[.] "DID YOU NOT KNOW THAT I MUST BE BUSY WITH MY FATHER'S AFFAIRS?" (2:49). BUT THEY DID NOT UNDERSTAND WHAT HE MEANT (2:50).

Our Lady thought Jesus was with Joseph, and Joseph

thought He was with her. All of a sudden they came together at a stopping point, and you can imagine Our Lady saying to Joseph, "Where's Jesus?"

He says, "I thought He was with you."

She says, "No, I thought He was with you."

"Well, He has to be around here somewhere, so let's look." So they're looking around and nobody saw Him.

Imagine going to the supermarket and there's a husband and wife. The wife thinks the little kid is with him, and he thinks the child is with her. What would they begin to feel? Guilty. They would feel responsible that they hadn't checked to see if their child was with one or the other. So Our Lady's first thought was probably that they had been negligent . . . or that the Pharisees had kidnapped Him, or that He had fallen somewhere and was injured perhaps.

It is likely that Our Dear Lord didn't tell her where He went so that she could experience the sense of loss. She was sinless but she wasn't Mrs. Omnipotent. All of that was part of her cross. She had to suffer everything any human being suffers in his or her interior life. Otherwise she would never understand. In fact, that's why Jesus came. He came to show us how to suffer, how to accept the uncertainties in our life, and that it's okay not to understand what He does or why. Otherwise you and I would never know that the darkness of faith is just as pleasing to God as the consolations of faith. In fact, the darkness of faith is what prunes you, detaches you, and makes you love God with a pure love. Consolations don't do that.

When you or I experience a sense of losing Jesus, we feel it terribly. And what do you ask yourself? "What did I do wrong? Did I sin in some way?" Or we treat God as if He has done us an injustice the moment we feel a lack of His presence, a lack of consolation, or a lack of knowledge.

Our Lady asks simply, "MY CHILD, WHY HAVE YOU DONE THIS TO US? SEE HOW WORRIED YOUR FATHER AND I HAVE BEEN, LOOKING FOR YOU" (2:48). In other words, "What did we do to displease you?" She placed the blame on herself. She would never have thought, "Look here now, I took care of You. I have believed in You. I said 'fiat' to the Father. I have fed You. Joseph taught You how to walk, and in spite of all that, why would You do this?" Now, a fallen, human mother would do that. But the Blessed Mother wanted to know if either she or Joseph had done some wrong in their hearts. Did they not love Him enough? Did they do something that made Him disappear for three solid days? What did they do? She would want to know so she would never do it again.

Parents don't feel that way when their kids disappear; they want to wallop them—"By God, when I get done with you, you'll never do that again." That wasn't Our Lady's attitude at all. Why did you *do this to us?* And He answered correctly, "DID YOU NOT KNOW THAT I MUST BE BUSY WITH MY FATHER'S AFFAIRS?" (2:49).

What did that response tell Mary? It told her that she hadn't done anything wrong—neither had Joseph. "You didn't disappoint Me," the Lord is telling her (I'm improvising here a little). "I was not displeased with you, but I had to give the teachers in the Temple a hint. I had to enlighten them in the Scriptures so that they would know I'm here, I'm coming." And they were astounded, it says, that He knew so much. You see, the first thing God would do is enlighten the doctors and the Church.

That incident did many wonderful things. It gave the Blessed Mother a real understanding of the sense of loss of God in her life. Our Lady, to be Queen of martyrs, Queen of confessors, Queen of virgins, Queen of everybody, had to go through every single kind of spiritual pain, physical pain, mental pain—she had to experience it along with her Son, Jesus.

Then it says He went down and was subject to them (Lk 2:51). He didn't do any more disappearing acts. But He was obliged, as God, to tell the Jews and the doctors, the Pharisees, the Sadducees, and the scribes first. Some of them must have wondered, "Well, there's His father, what's He talking about?" God speaks to us today as He spoke to those teachers, and to Our Lady, and to Saint Joseph: in mystery.

UNION WITH JESUS

Immersion in Scripture is a critical part of knowing Jesus. My whole religious life is bound up in the one reality of Jesus. The thrust of my entire life must be a profound union with Jesus—a union of my heart: to love like Him; a union of my memory: to remember the Father as He did; a union of my intellect: to be humble of heart, to see the world as He does in the Scriptures; and a union of my will: to see the Spirit moving and to follow wherever He leads. . . .

My union with God is uppermost and has to be the criteria by which I judge everything, because that's how I'll be judged at death. I shall only be judged by love. That's why I keep telling you to keep your eyes on the top of the mountain, to keep your eyes on the essence of Jesus and His wondrous, immense, fiery, burning love for you.

The Boldness of John the Baptist

❖

Matthew 14:3–4; John 1:19–23

John the Baptist was such a strong man. If you have a concept of humility as somehow being weak, or requiring you to become a doormat, you ought to look at John the Baptist. He was so bold. You know, he yelled at Herod (who was sleeping around with his brother's wife): "IT IS AGAINST THE LAW FOR YOU TO HAVE HER" (Mt 14:4). This is the king he's yelling at. Nobody, not the Pharisees, not the Sadducees, not the doctors, not the high priest, no one would tell Herod that he was wrong. When this group asked, "WHO ARE YOU?" (Jn 1:19) he could have, right then and there, said, "I'm a prophet." They asked, "ARE YOU THE PROPHET?" (1:21)—meaning the Messiah—and John answered, "No." "WHO ARE YOU?" they asked (1:22). He answered, "I AM, AS ISAIAH PROPHESIED: A VOICE THAT CRIES IN THE WILDERNESS: MAKE A STRAIGHT WAY FOR THE LORD" (1:23). What great strength.

Humble people are not patsies. When the time comes, and if the opportunity comes to give honor and glory to God, they are strong people. They are not going to back down either. So some of our overly pious concepts of humility are just ridiculous.

John knew Jesus and he was single-minded. Single-minded. That's what the saints are: single-minded. They have one thing in mind: the Lord. We stray. We go back and forth. Sometimes we are like a reed shaking in the wind. We alternate; we change our course every so often. Other things, other people, other events crowd in upon us, and they prevent us from keeping our mind on Jesus. But we've gotta keep pulling ourselves in, because of our poor human nature. We've gotta keep pulling ourselves in and pushing our egos aside.

That's why we need to pray to the Spirit—pray that we don't lose sight of why we're here, that we don't become loners or become distracted or fragmented—that we don't become a people who slowly push God to the periphery. We've got to be single-minded, like John.

People should never keep you from God, and neither should events. Nothing on this earth should keep you from the love of God. You have to strive to see the Lord in the present moment. You have a job to do; do it well and do it with love. If you have to deal with people, then see Jesus in those people, love them with the same love with which you love the Lord.

If you look at yourself you will find that 99 percent of the problems you have stem from your own will. We want things this way, we want this person this way, and we want this event this way. Well, life is not here to give you everything you want. Follow the Lord and be bold like John the Baptist—be bold with the world and with yourself and watch where He takes you.

The Baptism of Jesus

❖

Matthew 3:13–17; John 10:40–42

THEN JESUS APPEARED: HE CAME FROM GALILEE TO THE JOR-
DAN TO BE BAPTISED BY JOHN (Mt 3:13). JOHN TRIED TO DIS-
SUADE HIM. "IT IS I WHO NEED BAPTISM FROM YOU[,]" HE SAID[,]
"AND YET YOU COME TO ME!" (3:14).

BUT JESUS REPLIED, "LEAVE IT LIKE THIS FOR THE TIME BE-
ING; IT IS FITTING THAT WE SHOULD, IN THIS WAY, DO ALL THAT
RIGHTEOUSNESS DEMANDS." AT THIS, JOHN GAVE IN TO HIM
(3:15).

Our Lord had to be baptized in order to sanctify the water for all of us. He allowed Himself, the Sinless One, to be
baptized. He instituted the sacrament of Baptism, by being
baptized Himself. He instituted all of the seven sacraments;
that's why you can't change them and you can't add or subtract
anything from them. That's why women cannot be priests.
Whatever Jesus did, we must do. The only sacraments we can
have are those sacraments that He instituted. The Church has
no authority whatever to institute a sacrament. It cannot create one.

Anyway, as Adam and Eve closed heaven to the world, the
sacrament of Baptism opened heaven to the world. That's why
He said, "Unless you are baptized by water and the Spirit, you
shall not enter the kingdom of heaven." And baptism is an awesome, awesome gift. John had the baptism of repentance. His
baptism did not open the gates of heaven to anyone. He only
prepared the people by calling them to repentance. As SOON

AS JESUS WAS BAPTISED HE CAME UP FROM THE WATER, AND SUD-
DENLY THE HEAVENS OPENED AND HE SAW THE SPIRIT OF GOD
DESCENDING LIKE A DOVE AND COMING DOWN ON HIM (3:16).

AND A VOICE SPOKE FROM HEAVEN, "THIS IS MY SON, THE
BELOVED; MY FAVOUR RESTS ON HIM" (3:17). At that point,
heaven opened. The Father spoke and the Holy Spirit was
there (in the appearance of the dove)—you could say it was
the first "public appearance" of the Trinity. The Trinity, Who
was so angered by the sin of Adam and Eve, were pleased with
the coming of Jesus.

And before we move beyond John the Baptist, look at this
passage in the book of John: JESUS WENT BACK AGAIN TO THE
FAR SIDE OF THE JORDAN TO STAY IN THE DISTRICT WHERE JOHN
HAD ONCE BEEN BAPTISING (Jn 10:40). MANY PEOPLE WHO CAME
TO HIM THERE SAID, "JOHN GAVE NO SIGNS"—see here it is—
"BUT ALL HE SAID ABOUT THIS MAN WAS TRUE" (10:41); AND MANY
OF THEM BELIEVED IN HIM (10:42). So you can be a prophet and
not give signs. You can be holy and not give that kind of miraculous sign. That was certainly the way of John the Baptist—and
yet of all the men born of women, Jesus said, no one is as great
as John the Baptist (Mt 11:11). So John the Baptist was greater
than Moses, Abraham, Jeremiah, everybody. I've always felt
sorry for these humble prophets. Here's little John, skinny and
scrawny—I mean how much weight can you gain on locusts
and honey? He wore these smelly camel skins. He looked and
smelled like a prophet should look and smell. You know what
I mean? He was the greatest of all the prophets yet there's not
one sign from John. So that ought to encourage all of us peons,
you know. It's not necessary to have ecstatic prayer, or to have
visions or locutions; it's not necessary to go into ecstasy every
three minutes or to levitate. It's not necessary to heal and to
deliver and to do all of those things—have all those charisms.

It's only necessary to do God's will with love. That's it. And that's what John the Baptist did. He did God's will with love and zeal. That's it . . . lost his head in the process. His only sign was to say, "There He is" (Jn 1:36). "There is Jesus." And that was it. After that, chop, chop. He was finished.

Temptations in the Desert
❖
Luke 4:1–12

Saint Luke brings out very well the temptation of Our Dear Lord in the desert. I think it might be good to look at this for the simple reason that we are all going to be tempted. I don't care who you are. Our Dear Lord was tempted in His memory, intellect, and will. We are mostly tempted in our emotions, our imaginations, and our animal nature because that's where most people live. And those who are intellectuals often miss the boat completely, because they get all caught up in their own intellect, their own abilities to perform, their own ability to understand great mysteries or great truth. We get caught up in these faculties because we orient them to ourselves. Let's look at this.

FILLED WITH THE HOLY SPIRIT, JESUS LEFT THE JORDAN AND WAS LED BY THE SPIRIT THROUGH THE WILDERNESS (4:1), BEING TEMPTED THERE BY THE DEVIL FOR FORTY DAYS. DURING THAT TIME HE ATE NOTHING AND AT THE END HE WAS HUNGRY (4:2).

It says He was led by the Holy Spirit to be tempted by the devil for forty days without relief. In case you complain about your temptations, forget it. None of us has a decent temptation. I don't know what yours are, but I'll bet you don't have a decent temptation when compared to this.

Our Dear Lord during that time ate nothing. At the end of forty days, He was hungry. I'm hungry after one day, you know? Our Dear Lord went to the extreme in every kind of suffering—the ultimate.

THEN THE DEVIL SAID TO HIM, "IF YOU ARE THE SON OF GOD, TELL THIS STONE TO TURN INTO A LOAF" (4:3). I'll make a bet; if you had fasted for forty days and you passed a bakery, the bread odor alone would be enough to break you because we don't operate on a sense level, we operate on a smell level. We're like little puppies. You know, they don't love you. They love your odor!

The enemy did not really know for sure if this was the One he was looking for. And Jesus said, "MAN DOES NOT LIVE ON BREAD ALONE" (4:4). Now, Our Dear Lord, if you noticed, did not argue with the devil. It's only little women, and even dumber men, who argue with Satan. We're talking about an intelligence that's so far beyond ours. It's like a million Einsteins wrapped in one mind—and you're going to argue with him? You're out of your league, sweetheart. Our Lord Himself never argued with Satan. He could have said, "No, that's presumption," and explained it to him. But you can't explain anything to the devil, so the Lord didn't. He just stated the truth.

Now there's the temptation of His memory and His imagination—He was surely imagining good, fresh bread. But His memory is filled with the Father, so He knows the truth, and the truth is that we don't live by bread alone. He knocked that one right out of the ball park.

Now the devil is acting more like the devil. He goes for the intellect. LEADING HIM TO A HEIGHT, THE DEVIL SHOWED HIM IN A MOMENT OF TIME ALL THE KINGDOMS OF THE WORLD (4:5) AND

SAID TO HIM, "I WILL GIVE YOU ALL THIS POWER AND THE GLORY OF THESE KINGDOMS, FOR IT HAS BEEN COMMITTED TO ME AND I GIVE IT TO ANYONE I CHOOSE" (4:6).

Well, that's an explanation of what's going on today. People today are not powerful because they're smart. They're given that power by the enemy. He'll give you anything as long as he can have your soul forever in utter, total, absolute misery. That's the reward for obedience to him. "WORSHIP ME, THEN, AND IT SHALL ALL BE YOURS" (4:7). Once someone has agreed to those terms, you can't even talk to them—that kind of darkness is only enlightened by prayer.

Our Lord never answered the enemy except by quoting Scripture, and He was very brief. The Lord said, "YOU MUST WORSHIP THE LORD YOUR GOD, AND SERVE HIM ALONE" (4:8). So here you see the battle between the lying kingdom and the Truth. Remember when the Lord said to the Pharisees, you're like your father who was a liar from the beginning—from the beginning he was a liar because when he said, "I shall ascend to the throne of the Most High," he was lying, of course. He couldn't. He's a creature. He forgot that, so it was all a lie. From the beginning he was a liar, and we can lie to ourselves by believing the enemy.

Now, Satan's getting worse. He's going to test the Lord's will—and he's using Scripture. The devil MADE HIM STAND ON THE PARAPET OF THE TEMPLE (4:9)—the very height—[HE SAID,] "IF YOU ARE THE SON OF GOD"—see, that's what he's trying to figure out—"THROW YOURSELF DOWN FROM HERE (4:9), FOR SCRIPTURE SAYS: HE WILL PUT HIS ANGELS IN CHARGE OF YOU, TO GUARD YOU (4:10). Ah, now he's getting smart. The devil is beginning to quote Scripture. He said, "AND AGAIN: THEY WILL HOLD YOU UP ON THEIR HANDS IN CASE YOU HURT YOUR FOOT AGAINST A STONE" (4:11). He arrogantly quotes Scripture, showing off from the first moment, and the Lord says, "YOU MUST NOT PUT THE LORD YOUR GOD TO THE TEST" (4:12). Three cheers.

This last sentence I think is so good. HAVING EXHAUSTED ALL THESE WAYS OF TEMPTING HIM, THE DEVIL LEFT HIM, TO RETURN AT THE APPOINTED TIME (4:13). So Our Dear Lord's faculties were tempted—"big-time," as you say today. We haven't gotten past our imaginations as far as the enemy is concerned. What are you proud of? Tell me. Your intellect? Your appearance? Your power? The enemy is ever watchful for an opening, so fill yourself with holiness and truth and persevere in that truth as Jesus did.

Ways of Fasting

❖

Mark 2:18–20

What does it mean to fast? It means to do without. It can be food, it can be things. Poverty is also a type of fasting. For example, if I'm hungry, I would love to have two pieces of bread smothered with a steak, or baloney, or a hamburger. That's what I would like. It may be what I visualize, but I deny myself—so what am I doing? I am doing without, see? The whole concept of fasting and poverty is to do without.

All fasting, poverty, obedience, humility—all of the virtues have everything to do with *doing without*. If I'm humble, I do without my pride. If I'm obedient, I do without my will. If I'm poor, I do without things. Doing without suddenly makes you possess all of those virtues: obedience, humility, poverty, and freedom. What an amazing thing.

Let's read this little bit on fasting in the Scripture. SOME

PEOPLE CAME AND SAID TO HIM, "WHY IS IT THAT JOHN'S DIS-
CIPLES AND THE DISCIPLES OF THE PHARISEES FAST, BUT YOUR
DISCIPLES DO NOT?" (2:18). JESUS REPLIED, "SURELY THE BRIDE-
GROOM'S ATTENDANTS WOULD NEVER THINK OF FASTING WHILE
THE BRIDEGROOM IS STILL WITH THEM? AS LONG AS THEY HAVE
THE BRIDEGROOM WITH THEM, THEY COULD NOT THINK OF FAST-
ING (2:19). BUT THE TIME WILL COME FOR THE BRIDEGROOM TO
BE TAKEN AWAY FROM THEM, AND THEN, ON THAT DAY, THEY WILL
FAST" (2:20).

Do you realize what He is saying? Right away we think
they're going to eat while Jesus is around and they're not going to eat when He's gone. That isn't what He's saying. Did
they not fast in the most awesome way when Our Dear Lord
was taken away from them? The privilege of getting up in the
morning and looking at His face, of seeing Him all day long,
of hearing the words of the Son of God, of going to bed at
night and knowing that in the morning they would see Him
there—all that was taken from them. Is that the fasting that
Our Lord meant when He said, "the Bridegroom will be taken
away from them and on that day they will fast"? You bet. Isn't
that what aridity is: the absence of God's consolation, the absence of spiritual feeling? Isn't that the source of so many of
our problems? Is that not like the Bridegroom leaving you?

So ask yourself sometime as you examine your conscience
(and I hope you do at least once a day at some point), when
you have a problem, ask yourself, "What is the source of this?"
And I'll make a bet it'll be one thing: You cannot do without.
You can't do without a wonderful consolation from God or a
wonderful light. You cannot do without food, you cannot do
without electricity, you cannot do without compliments, and
you cannot do without your own will: You cannot do without!
I think if we examined ourselves on that one point, we would

understand fasting. It seems to me that virtue is intimately tied to that understanding.

I've seen some terribly penitential people when it came to food, and they were impossibly hard to get along with. I'm not knocking fasting from food, I'm just saying that it is only one way to fast; there are other ways. If we fasted from our will, for instance, or from our vanity; those are awesome ways to fast. Try it sometime.

Miracle of the Loaves and the Fishes

❖

Mark 6:39–40; John 6:9, 12–13

Saint Mark says there was plenty of grass in that place. THEN [JESUS] ORDERED THEM TO GET ALL THE PEOPLE TOGETHER IN GROUPS ON THE GREEN GRASS (Mk 6:39), AND THEY SAT DOWN ON THE GROUND IN SQUARES OF HUNDREDS AND FIFTIES (6:40).

That's why I like Saint Mark; he gives us all these little details. He's like a set maker. Well, if you can imagine how tall the grass must have been in those days. It had to be as high as this table. And you have to think of five thousand people sitting in squares. Now why the Lord asked them to assemble in squares, nobody knows. He just didn't say put them aside; He said put the people in squares of hundreds and fifties. This was a job; it took time to count everybody out in squares. So you've got all these people sitting in squares and all of a sudden the apostles start going out and distributing baskets of fish that's already cooked, I'm sure. Because don't forget there's a little portion of this miracle that we easily overlook: it was cooked fish the Lord multiplied.

The Scripture tells us in John: "THERE IS A SMALL BOY . . . WITH FIVE BARLEY LOAVES AND TWO FISH" (6:9). The boy couldn't carry raw fish around for three days. It would have been stinking. He had dried fish. So what the Lord multiplied was dried fish, not fresh fish. It must have been like baccalà. The Italians used to hang fish up and it would dry until it was like a board. Then you dropped it in water and it would fluff up and get thick. Just beautiful. The bread the Lord broke must have been stale, but I'm sure what He distributed was fresh. Look at me focusing on the menu. . . .

Anyway, there were a lot of people there, lots of children. You can imagine how they were eating. This was not a brunch at the Ritz. They're sloppy. They're caressing their food, it's all over their hands, it's all over their clothes—it's everywhere. It's a mess. It's important for us to understand the utter chaos and mess it must have been.

And what does the Lord say to do? What does He say? "PICK UP THE PIECES LEFT OVER, SO THAT NOTHING GETS WASTED" (6:12). SO THEY PICKED THEM UP, AND FILLED TWELVE HAMPERS WITH SCRAPS LEFT OVER FROM THE MEAL (6:13). *Pick up the pieces.* Pick up everything that's left. He was so interested in picking this stuff up. What do you think happened to this slop? I'll bet the apostles ate it for days and days, like that Thanksgiving turkey you eat until New Year's. Symbolically this is a foreshadowing of the Eucharist: not one particle of it is to be left behind. Every fragment must be consumed.

There is a lesson in those fragments lying there in the grass. In our lives we take something God gives us that is good and we turn it into garbage. We fragment it. We pull it apart.

We scatter it all over the place. Sin kind of squashes it, or just destroys it, or makes it ugly. God is saying to us, "Don't throw it away. I'm going to make it nourishing for you, even in this state."

Your life and my life are full of scraps that we would like to hide in the tall grass. But we can't. Look, I have a tendency to temper, I have a tendency to jealousy, I have a tendency to impatience, I have a tendency to be overly sensitive. Now we think, "I know I have these failings, so I'm going to pray and they're going to go away." That's not necessarily true. We won't know until we die and face God how even the failures of our lives have been used by Him, and transformed by His power for our good. Isn't that great? God can grow roses on your garbage heap. He can actually use your scraps. Don't toss them away. Give them to the Lord.

A Different Vision of Heaven

❖

Matthew 22:23–32

THAT DAY SOME SADDUCEES—WHO DENY THAT THERE IS A RESURRECTION—APPROACHED HIM AND THEY PUT THIS QUESTION TO HIM (22:23), "MASTER, MOSES SAID THAT IF A MAN DIES CHILDLESS, HIS BROTHER IS TO MARRY THE WIDOW, HIS SISTER-IN-LAW, TO RAISE CHILDREN FOR HIS BROTHER" (22:24)— they're always trying to trick the Lord—"NOW WE HAD A CASE INVOLVING SEVEN BROTHERS; THE FIRST MARRIED AND THEN DIED WITHOUT CHILDREN, LEAVING HIS WIFE TO HIS BROTHER" (22:25). It goes on and on like that, and eventually all seven brothers marry this poor woman. "NOW AT THE RESURRECTION TO WHICH OF THOSE SEVEN WILL SHE BE WIFE?" (22:28). Isn't that a clever question? Jesus says: "YOU ARE WRONG, BECAUSE YOU UNDERSTAND NEITHER THE SCRIPTURES NOR THE POWER OF GOD (22:29). FOR AT THE RESURRECTION MEN AND WOMEN DO NOT MARRY; NO, THEY ARE LIKE THE ANGELS IN HEAVEN" (22:30).

This is a very good place to stop and meditate, because Jesus is saying that heaven is vastly different from what we imagine. You're not going to need all the people you need here to make you happy. We will love everyone there and we will be loved by everyone there, but we definitely will not be the same as we are here. Because no matter what state of life you're in now, it's the place where you're tested, proven, purified for the kingdom, and your entire glory forever and ever depends on what you do in this place.

And He said, "AT THE RESURRECTION MEN AND WOMEN DO NOT MARRY; NO, THEY ARE LIKE THE ANGELS IN HEAVEN (22:30). AND AS FOR THE RESURRECTION OF THE DEAD, HAVE YOU NEVER READ WHAT GOD HIMSELF SAID TO YOU (22:31): I AM THE GOD OF ABRAHAM, THE GOD OF ISAAC, AND THE GOD OF JACOB? GOD IS GOD, NOT OF THE DEAD, BUT OF THE LIVING" (22:32).

So He taught them two lessons. First, the reason we cling to earth is because we're so attached to people, to things, to our opinions, to ourselves, and we cannot imagine life without any of this. And second, the purpose of life is to get you to a place where you love everybody, accept everything in order to purify yourself, so that you may arrive at that place in the kingdom God has destined for you.

The Woman at the Well

❖

John 4:5–29

Please understand that I have my own personal rendition of Scripture, but it helps me and I hope it helps you. You've got to put fire and life into your reading of the Scripture—use your imagination and live it. Don't just sit there and read it like a newspaper. It is Someone, not something.

It says here, ON THE WAY HE CAME TO THE SAMARITAN TOWN CALLED SYCHAR, NEAR THE LAND THAT JACOB GAVE TO HIS SON JOSEPH (4:5). JACOB'S WELL IS THERE AND JESUS, TIRED BY THE JOURNEY, SAT STRAIGHT DOWN BY THE WELL. IT WAS ABOUT THE SIXTH HOUR (4:6).

Can you imagine God being tired? Can you imagine anyone loving you so much that He wants to feel what you feel? Before redemption we might have said to God, "Have you ever been persecuted and hated and treated unjustly, when You didn't know where to go or where to turn?" But now we have a glorious God Who knows. He knows what it is to be lonely, to be rejected, to be tired. I appreciate that because I rise and go to bed tired. When I am most tired I think of Him, and unite my fatigue with His, and somehow there is enough strength for another hour, another day.

So here it is the sixth hour and the Samaritan woman came to draw water. Now, no decent woman drew water at noontime. She was ostracized by the women of the village, so she came when there was no one around. Imagine her tiredness. JESUS SAID TO HER, "GIVE ME A DRINK" (4:7). Oh that was a no-no. No Jew asked a Samaritan for anything, but Jesus was free and he said, "GIVE ME A DRINK." The woman did exactly what we do to God: She questioned Him. We have the impression that if God knew us He would not love us. That's sick. Let me burst your bubble. Not only does He know what you've done, He knows what you might have done—and He still loves you.

THE SAMARITAN WOMAN SAID TO HIM, "WHAT? YOU ARE A JEW AND YOU ASK ME, A SAMARITAN, FOR A DRINK?"—JEWS, IN FACT, DO NOT ASSOCIATE WITH SAMARITANS (4:9). JESUS RE-PLIED: "IF YOU ONLY KNEW WHAT GOD IS OFFERING AND WHO IT IS THAT IS SAYING TO YOU: GIVE ME A DRINK, YOU WOULD HAVE BEEN THE ONE TO ASK, AND HE WOULD HAVE GIVEN YOU LIVING WATER" (4:10). And what does she do? Just what you and I would do. "YOU HAVE NO BUCKET, SIR," SHE ANSWERED (4:11).

"You don't have a bucket." God just gave her the words of eternal life, and she says, "You don't have a bucket." And you do the same thing. You say to God, "Look at what I did twenty years ago. You couldn't love me." She then tries to educate God. She says, "THE WELL IS DEEP: HOW COULD YOU GET THIS LIVING WATER? (4:11). ARE YOU A GREATER MAN THAN OUR FA-THER JACOB WHO GAVE US THIS WELL AND DRANK FROM IT HIM-

SELF WITH HIS SONS AND HIS CATTLE?" (4:12). See, she's trying to talk God out of his love. JESUS REPLIED: "WHOEVER DRINKS THIS WATER WILL GET THIRSTY AGAIN (4:13); BUT ANYONE WHO DRINKS THE WATER THAT I SHALL GIVE WILL NEVER BE THIRSTY AGAIN: THE WATER THAT I SHALL GIVE WILL TURN INTO A SPRING INSIDE HIM, WELLING UP TO ETERNAL LIFE" (4:14). You know what she says? "Lay it on me Lord." She says, "SIR, . . . GIVE ME SOME OF THAT WATER, SO THAT I MAY NEVER GET THIRSTY AND NEVER HAVE TO COME HERE AGAIN TO DRAW WATER" (4:15). She was probably thinking about all those gossipy women staring at her from their tents every time she went to the well. That's what we tell God: "If You love me, then You will give me all these good things." But the good things in life are those that are sometimes the most painful, because they mold and shape and transform us.

The Lord says, "GO AND CALL YOUR HUSBAND . . . AND COME BACK HERE" (4:16). Ah, here comes the truth. THE WOMAN ANSWERED, "I HAVE NO HUSBAND." HE SAID TO HER, "YOU ARE RIGHT TO SAY, 'I HAVE NO HUSBAND' (4:17); FOR ALTHOUGH YOU HAVE HAD FIVE, THE ONE YOU HAVE NOW IS NOT YOUR HUSBAND. YOU SPOKE THE TRUTH THERE" (4:18). You know, I can see Jesus with a little smile sometimes, and I think He had one here. I just don't believe that He didn't smile from time to time—there is no way that He could live with Peter and not laugh.

"I SEE YOU ARE A PROPHET, SIR[,]" SAID THE WOMAN (4:19). "OUR FATHERS WORSHIPPED ON THIS MOUNTAIN . . ." (4:20). What has that to do with anything? The God-Man has read her soul, and what has she done? Changed the subject! What happens to you when something comes along that draws out the worst in you? You blame everybody, you blame the economy, circumstances, you just get it away from yourself. Then you don't have to carry the cross—you don't have to imitate the

Passion, you just blame it on everybody else and go your way. So this woman changes the subject. She says, "OUR FATHERS WORSHIPPED ON THIS MOUNTAIN, WHILE YOU SAY THAT JERUSALEM IS THE PLACE WHERE ONE OUGHT TO WORSHIP" (4:20). But He didn't say that. He said, "You have five husbands and one is not your own!" She is the great hedger, but Jesus goes along with her.

JESUS SAID: "BELIEVE ME, WOMAN, THE HOUR IS COMING WHEN YOU WILL WORSHIP THE FATHER NEITHER ON THIS MOUNTAIN NOR IN JERUSALEM (4:21). YOU WORSHIP WHAT YOU DO NOT KNOW; WE WORSHIP WHAT WE DO KNOW; FOR SALVATION COMES FROM THE JEWS (4:22). BUT THE HOUR WILL COME—IN FACT IT IS HERE ALREADY—WHEN TRUE WORSHIPPERS WILL WORSHIP THE FATHER IN SPIRIT AND TRUTH: THAT IS THE KIND OF WORSHIPPER THE FATHER WANTS (4:23). GOD IS SPIRIT, AND THOSE WHO WORSHIP MUST WORSHIP IN SPIRIT AND TRUTH" (4:24). But she still will not admit what she is.

THE WOMAN SAID TO HIM, "I KNOW THAT MESSIAH—THAT IS, CHRIST—IS COMING; AND WHEN HE COMES HE WILL TELL US EVERYTHING" (4:25). Do you see what she is doing? She will not admit what is wrong with her. She is negating the necessity of humility, of pain, of truth. She can't take looking at herself.

Jesus says: "I WHO AM SPEAKING TO YOU . . . I AM HE" (4:26). Imagine the healing that must have gone on in that woman's soul. The one Messiah that the prophets spoke of and promised is speaking to a sinner and asking for love. He still asks us for love; yours and mine. He is trying to shape and mold you through the battles all about us, internal and external. We need Jesus and He says to you and me, "I am He."

AT THIS POINT HIS DISCIPLES RETURNED, AND WERE SURPRISED TO FIND HIM SPEAKING TO A WOMAN, THOUGH NONE OF THEM ASKED, "WHAT DO YOU WANT FROM HER?" OR, "WHY ARE

YOU TALKING TO HER?" (4:27). (They were too chicken to ask about it.)

Look what happens to this woman. THE WOMAN PUT DOWN HER WATER JAR AND HURRIED BACK TO THE TOWN TO TELL THE PEOPLE (4:28), "COME AND SEE A MAN WHO HAS TOLD ME EVERYTHING I EVER DID; I WONDER IF HE IS THE CHRIST?" (4:29). She began to see clearly all the things in her life that were opposed to Christ. She compared herself not to the other women in the village, but to Jesus. The light of Jesus made her understand who and what she was, and there was no fear in admitting it. The people started coming out of the town and started walking toward Him.

Meanwhile, the apostles came back and they WERE URGING HIM, "RABBI, DO HAVE SOMETHING TO EAT" (4:32); BUT HE SAID, "I HAVE FOOD TO EAT THAT YOU DO NOT KNOW ABOUT" (4:32). Then He went on to tell them the very thing I want you to remember this week: JESUS SAID: "MY FOOD IS TO DO THE WILL OF THE ONE WHO SENT ME, AND TO COMPLETE HIS WORK" (4:34).

Our food is to do God's will each day, each moment. To look at ourselves with humility and say, "There is nothing in me that is of any value. I am a sinner. I have to struggle and fight to be good, and every morning I begin again and every evening I have to ask forgiveness for all the failings of my day." You never go anywhere without Him. He suffers when you suffer. He delights when you delight. I never see a crowd that my heart does not go out to tell them how much He loves us. I never look at an adulterer or a blasphemer when I don't think, "I wish they knew the love of Jesus." Be childlike with God. Have compassion for His pain, for your brother and yourself. Have the love of the Spirit in your heart because God lives in you and loves you, and you must give that love to others.

Walking on Water

❖

Matthew 14:22–33

J ESUS MADE THE DISCIPLES GET INTO THE BOAT AND GO ON
AHEAD TO THE OTHER SIDE WHILE HE WOULD SEND THE
CROWDS AWAY (14:22). AFTER SENDING THE CROWDS AWAY HE
WENT UP INTO THE HILLS BY HIMSELF TO PRAY. WHEN EVENING
CAME, HE WAS THERE ALONE (14:23), WHILE THE BOAT, BY NOW
FAR OUT ON THE LAKE, WAS BATTLING WITH A HEAVY SEA, FOR
THERE WAS A HEAD-WIND (14:24).

Now, this is the beginning of the night. Jesus prays and
He's watching. He's watching you and me in this age. Nothing
is hidden from Him. Everything is now. He sees us. Even at
that time, He saw us here examining His Word. He also saw
the apostles and they were battling.

He watched them until the fourth watch—anywhere from
three to six a.m. He's just sitting there watching them. With
Jesus there is always a test: there is a pain, an ache, there
is something you don't like to do, or something you find very
hard. And all the while He just watches. It's a great help for
us to understand that we should never deliberately disappoint
Him by doing something goofy or saying no outright, because
He's watching you, all your life.

Now, IN THE FOURTH WATCH OF THE NIGHT HE WENT TO-
WARDS THEM, WALKING ON THE LAKE (14:25), AND WHEN THE
DISCIPLES SAW HIM WALKING ON THE LAKE THEY WERE TERRI-
FIED (14:26). Now you would think they would say, "Wow, look
at that," or, "He must be the Lord, who else could walk on

water?" But they were terrified. His water walk didn't seem to have the result He intended.

Jesus was trying to prove that He was the Son of God. And instead they were frightened out of their minds. What did they say? "Oh, hi-ya, Jesus, thank you for coming. Boy, you're wonderful. We didn't know You could walk on water." Nope. They said: "IT IS A GHOST" (14:26). Ha-ha. Oh, dear Jesus, a ghost! What kind of ghost would walk on water? And why would a ghost be going toward them?

See, they missed the whole point of the miracle. I wonder, very often, how many of those points I've missed in my own life. God loves you to go out on a limb and even though it gets shaky—He loves you to do that so that He can perform a miracle. Would God have walked on the water had there not been a storm? Scripture tells us that the Lord watched their reaction and then when they were scared out of their wits and no longer trusted in themselves and their own capability to steer the ship—He came. Many times that's when He comes to us as well.

AT ONCE JESUS CALLED OUT TO THEM, SAYING, "COURAGE! IT IS I! DO NOT BE AFRAID" (14:27). You know, if we realized that Our Dear Lord watches us, every one of us individually, as He watched those apostles in that boat, every moment, whether you're awake or asleep, you would love Him and prefer Him to all things. He watches you, not as a Judge, but as One who loves us so much. We don't catch it. We're terrified. We're busy with so many things. And what does He say to us? "Courage! It's I. Don't be afraid." We worry about the past, we worry about the future, and we worry about the present. Instead we should be saying, "He's watching me. He sees me and He loves me."

IT WAS PETER WHO ANSWERED—now here comes the great tester. They're looking at Him, He's walking on the water, and what does Peter say? "Well, if it is You, let me test You." Aren't we strange people? Many of us are so proud we do the same thing. It's a wonder the Lord doesn't just wipe us off the face of the earth. We test God, just as Peter does here. "Lord," he said, "If it is you, tell me to come to you across the water" (14:28).

And the Lord said, "Come." Then Peter got out of the boat (14:29)—listen to what he's doing: he gets out of the boat and he starts walking across the water. You know, I sometimes wonder how many miracles we begin and then ruin by our own inaction or fear. Do you ever wonder that?

I always pray, "Lord, don't let me chicken out if You have something hard for me to do." The Lord said, "Come," but as soon as [Peter] felt the force of the wind, he took fright and began to sink (14:30). Peter is on the water and he is walking on it. His feet are wet, but he's walking on the water. And all of a sudden, a big wind comes and he loses his faith. He was distracted from the gaze of Jesus. It was the wind that got him—the world, his knowledge of the world. And so he sank. He started going down.

What does he say now? "Lord! Save me!" (14:30). At least he was smart enough to know he needed the Lord—as we need Him today. We need to say when we're weak, when we're lost, when we're disappointed, when we're just worn out, "Lord, save me." You think, "Well, I'll never walk on water." Oh, I think we do that often, and we sink because we feel the power of the world, the power of people, the power of everybody and everything. . . . That's why nothing is changing in the world, because nobody has the courage of faith. Nobody.

And Jesus put out his hand at once and held him. "Man of little faith," he said[,] "why did you doubt?" (14:31). Couldn't Our Lord say that now about us? Now you say, "Wait a minute. Peter was told to walk on the water and he did it. He felt the wind, and the wind was pretty hard. It can knock you over. It destroys buildings. Peter was afraid, so he called out." All that is pretty logical, very logical. But what does the Lord answer to something that looks that logical and that reasonable and that right? "MAN OF LITTLE FAITH, . . . WHY DID YOU DOUBT?" (14:31). See, God doesn't think like you. He doesn't want your excuses. He nailed it.

There was absolutely no human excuse for Jesus: you have no faith and why do you doubt? AND AS THEY GOT INTO THE BOAT THE WIND DROPPED (14:32). THE MEN IN THE BOAT BOWED DOWN BEFORE HIM AND SAID—what He wanted to hear— "TRULY, YOU ARE THE SON OF GOD" (14:33). It took failure, fear, and humiliation to give them light. And that's true with us too. Sometimes it takes all of that to give us light.

HALOS

The mistake we make when we read the Scriptures is we put a halo on these men before it was there. We look at every man in the Gospel from afar with great yearning in our heart to be holy and we think, "Oh that's not for me." But God is looking for people willing to accept themselves where they are, and strive for holiness. There is no perfection in this world. But there is holiness.

The Greatest?

❖

Mark 9:33–35

J ust imagine twelve unknown, dummy fishermen. The only intellectual was Judas. He was a Judean and the only Judean in the crowd. Shrewd man—that shrewdness did him in. The rest of them weren't too bright. Suffering wasn't even a consideration for them, especially when they were with the Master. When Jesus would speak before the crowds the apostles were strutting around him, looking out at the crowds, thinking: "Don't you wish you were up here?" They acted very smart.

When Our Lord explained the parables they stood there as if they understood. Then at night they would say, "Master, explain the parable to us. What did you mean?" They were too proud to ask in front of the crowd. They lacked simplicity; they were proud, ambitious.

Now, would you have chosen people to be teachers who didn't understand simple things? You wouldn't, but the Lord did, to show His power—the power to overcome their weakness. He does the same with us, if we let Him. The apostles were faulty men.

When the apostles were fussing over which one of them would be the greatest, the Lord very gently looked at them, and He said, "WHAT WERE YOU ARGUING ABOUT ON THE ROAD?"(9:33). They hemmed and hawed as men often do. I can see the gleam in the Lord's eye. I imagine James and John must have been the worst. They were called Sons of Thunder because their father had a hot temper and so did they. I'll bet James and John said, "Jesus prefers us because when He went to Jurius's daughter's house, you know who He took with Him." The other apostles were probably infuriated with these guys. Our Lord looks at them and says, "IF ANYONE WANTS TO BE FIRST, HE MUST MAKE HIMSELF LAST OF ALL AND SERVANT OF ALL" (9:35). This was before Pentecost. After Pentecost there was such a change in these men. They would learn what being a "SERVANT OF ALL" really meant. That's the amazing thing about the Holy Spirit: He transforms—today and always.

THE APOSTLES DIDN'T GET IT EITHER

If you ever feel discouraged that you don't understand the Scriptures and you say, "Oh if I could have just sat there and listened to the Lord and looked at Him, and watched Him . . ." Well, the apostles were there and they apparently never caught on. They were always in another world.

So sometimes you ought to pray to one of the apostles and say, "Look, you know how it is when you don't understand what the Lord is doing or saying in your life, pray for me, so that I will understand."

Calming the Storm

❖

Mark 4:35–41

Mark gives us so many little details. When Jesus was asleep in the boat with the apostles, Mark tells us He had His head on a cushion. Sound asleep. Storms, I understand in that region of the world, come up very quickly. They're rough storms. They're not like little breezes. They're real rough windstorms.

WITH THE COMING OF EVENING THAT SAME DAY, HE SAID TO THEM, "LET US CROSS OVER TO THE OTHER SIDE" (4:35). AND LEAVING THE CROWD BEHIND THEY TOOK HIM, JUST AS HE WAS, IN THE BOAT (4:36). That's an interesting phrase. I wonder what JUST AS HE WAS means? Did they have one of those "come as you are" parties? I never did figure that out.

THEN IT BEGAN TO BLOW A GALE (4:37). This isn't an ordinary windstorm, it's a gale. AND THE WAVES WERE BREAKING INTO THE BOAT SO THAT IT WAS ALMOST SWAMPED (4:37). The waves are now going into the boat, over the boat, and almost sinking the boat. THEY WOKE HIM—but, it says—HE WAS IN THE STERN, HIS HEAD ON A CUSHION, ASLEEP (4:38). THEY WOKE HIM AND SAID TO HIM, "MASTER, DO YOU NOT CARE? WE'RE GOING DOWN!" Boy. AND HE WOKE UP AND REBUKED THE WIND AND SAID TO THE SEA, "QUIET NOW! BE CALM!" AND THE WIND DROPPED (4:39). Boom. No wind.

It's amazing to me how the Lord took care of the storm first—but it always makes me think: God does answer my prayers, but I sometimes wonder if He is disappointed in me when He answers them. This is a sure case of God answering the apostles' prayers, but He was also rather disappointed in them. Because after He rebuked the wind and said, "QUIET NOW. BE CALM!" and the wind dropped, and all of that, He looked at them and said, "WHY ARE YOU SO FRIGHTENED. HOW IS IT THAT YOU HAVE NO FAITH?" (4:40). He didn't say, "How is it you have little faith?" It's "How is it you have NO faith?"

I want you to really study that for a minute. You're in a boat, the waters are coming over, they're filling the boat. You're getting buckets, and you're trying to get the water out. But as fast as you get one bucket out, twenty-five more come in. The boat is getting heavy, it's beginning to sink, and the One who created the whole thing is lying in the stern of the boat fast asleep. What's your reaction? Had the apostles just kept bucketing it out, I think they would have made it. That's what He was trying to tell them when He said, "Why are you frightened?" In other words, when you're faced with a situation and you're fighting it, keep on fighting! "HOW IS IT THAT YOU HAVE NO FAITH?"

They should have said something else besides, "Master, we're drowning. Don't you care?" To say that God doesn't care is to lack faith—totally—and that's why they were frightened. The apostles lost it when they thought He didn't care about them. They said: "MASTER, DO YOU NOT CARE? WE'RE GOING DOWN!" And the Lord was rebuking this ridiculous idea.

As I said before, I think if they would have just kept bucketing and working hard to get the water out, even though it may have been a couple of coffee cans, they would have been fine. Jesus never sleeps, even when you think otherwise.

And look at what the apostles say afterward. They're all excited over the miracle. THEY WERE FILLED WITH AWE AND SAID TO ONE ANOTHER, "WHO CAN THIS BE? EVEN THE WIND AND THE

SEA OBEY HIM" (4:41). So obviously at this point they were not ready to accept Him as Lord—they were just learning about Him. But learning or not, He upbraided them for not having any faith.

It's an interesting paragraph because it contains so much of our human nature. According to your personalities, you can see what your reaction would be—each one of you. What would you have done in the same situation? What do you do when the storms are sinking your boat? When you get so frightened during life's storms, threatened, and unhappy, do you really believe that Jesus is the Son of God? Is there a purpose in His allowing the storm in your life?

A Sinner Repents (A Meditation)

❖

Luke 7:36–50

These "Journeys into Scripture" are really a chance to practice mental prayer. We use our mind, the faculties of our soul, our memory, our imagination, our will, and our understanding during these "Journeys."

We're going to Jerusalem, and we go to the house of one Simon the Pharisee. We see the Master and His twelve apostles coming into the room. There's a large table there, a very long one, and some semicircular tables. There are couches jutting out and we realize they are reclining at table.

I look at Simon the Pharisee; he's a tall man with a beard. He has a habit of stroking his beard especially when he's in deep thought. His eyes are narrow. He's a nervous man. And as Christ walks in, he scans Him from head to toe. I look at

Christ and I know that He knows He was not invited out of love; He was invited out of hatred. They want to see who this Jesus is, to test Him, to ridicule Him, to make Him look a fool. Christ goes and He takes His place at table. Christ is tall and handsome, and though He looks majestic and kingly, He is so humble and approachable.

I see the apostles and they look a little uneasy. They know why they were invited and they dislike these kinds of dinners. They would much rather be out with the Master under a tree, alone. But the Master is very serene and He looks around, and unlike the apostles, He is in full possession of His peace. I think to myself, "In this circumstance, what would I do? Would I be so conscious of what the men who invited me were thinking and why they invited me?" I look at Christ and He sees this as an opportunity to show love for His Father. His Father permits it, and He accepts it.

Finally the meal begins and the servants are passing the food and all of a sudden there is a silence in the room. A great hush. Through the door comes a woman, a very beautiful woman with long black hair, striking. Simon looks at her and he leans over to his neighbor and he whispers in his ear.

There's Peter and he's looking at her with an odd expression on his face. It seems to say, "Oh no, I hope she's not going to do what I think she's going to do." She makes her way toward the Savior—she seems completely oblivious of everyone in the room, except Jesus. She goes to Him, kneels at the end of the couch where He's reclining, and she begins to cry. Her sobs fill the room. No one moves a muscle. As she cries, her tears fall on Our Lord's feet, so many of them that His feet are soon wet. She takes her long beautiful hair and she begins to dry them and she kisses them with great affection. I feel so sorry for her. I look at Simon the Pharisee. Simon is lost in thought. His eyes narrow and he strokes his beard and says, "IF THIS MAN WERE A PROPHET HE WOULD KNOW WHO THIS WOMAN IS THAT IS TOUCHING HIM AND WHAT A BAD NAME SHE HAS" (7:39).

Jesus is looking at the woman with great love and compassion. He glances over to the Pharisee and says, "SIMON . . . YOU SEE THIS WOMAN?" (7:44). (And I think to myself, "Who hasn't!") He says, "Have you seen this woman, Simon? When I CAME INTO YOUR HOUSE, YOU POURED NO WATER OVER MY FEET" (7:44). I suddenly realize that Simon skipped the Lord. It was the custom in those days for the host to kneel down and wash the feet of those invited to dinner. They put oil on their beards and gave their guests a kiss. This custom was omitted for Christ deliberately.

Jesus said, "[THIS WOMAN] HAS POURED OUT HER TEARS OVER MY FEET AND WIPED THEM AWAY WITH HER HAIR (7:44). SIMON YOU GAVE ME NO KISS" (7:45). I think to myself, Can it be that God's Son missed the kiss of one like Simon? A proud, arrogant, egotistical man whose one design was to humiliate Him? Could He miss the kiss of one like this? Is that an example of God's infinite love for me? He yearned for the kiss of a traitor, from one who hated Him. But God loved that much.

Jesus said, "This woman, Simon, has not ceased to kiss my feet. And I say to thee, her many sins are forgiven her because she loved much." And I think, Is that all, Lord? Is that all we must do? She didn't even ask forgiveness, she just loved much. As I look at this scene I see the mercy of God making one person bitter and filling another with joy. "My Lord," I say, "I kneel with this sinner at Thy feet. You know what's in my heart. You know Lord that I try and I fail and I try and I fail and I love Thee with all my heart. With all my heart."

The Master looks down at me and He says, "Go in peace, daughter. Thy sins are forgiven thee. Have joy. For I love thee with an everlasting love (Jer 31:3). I have called thee by thy name, thou art mine" (Is 43:1). And so for a few moments, let each one of us kneel at the feet of Christ and tell Him what's on our hearts.

The Truth (And Your Own Business) Shall Set You Free

❖

John 8:31–32

To the Jews who believed in him Jesus said: "If you make my word your home you will indeed be my disciples (8:31), you will learn the truth and the truth will make you free" (8:32).

Be careful of worldly truth! I've told you that a thousand times. The world loves to say that the truth will make you free. The only truth that makes you free is the truth of Jesus. But there are many other truths that can make you proud, make you despair, make you hopeless, make you discouraged, make you morose, make you sad. You need the truth that will make you mind your own business.

Remember that little saying I put up there, Mind your own business. If you all got that one practical thing, setting aside anything spiritual, you would be holy today—by noon. By noon you would be holy if you would just mind your own business. You'd be surprised at how little business you actually have. You'd be shocked to find that your business is so tiny, and that you crowd your mind with everybody else's. It's no good for you spiritually or otherwise. You have very little business, honey.

Trusting Providence

❖

Matthew 6:25–33

There's a beautiful chapter here on trust in Saint Matthew's Gospel, it advises us never to worry about anything. See, this constant worry. Our Lord said one time, "CAN ANY ONE OF YOU, FOR ALL HIS WORRYING, ADD ONE SINGLE CUBIT TO HIS SPAN OF LIFE?" (6:27). See, you can't. Worrying is not an act of trust. Concern, even, is not an act of trust. Thinking you have to do something about this or that is not an act of trust. If we're asked to do anything, just do it! Trust means to trust the world to God, to trust the outcome of our works to God, to trust our day to God, to trust our families to God. It means: Drop it. Drop it. Do you understand? We can't drop things. We've just got to hold on to them. We Americans, for instance, are do-it-yourselfers; and that is an absolute tragedy because you cannot advance in holiness without trust.

Look at what the Lord says in Matthew:

"THAT IS WHY I AM TELLING YOU NOT TO WORRY ABOUT YOUR LIFE AND WHAT YOU ARE TO EAT, NOR ABOUT YOUR BODY AND HOW YOU ARE TO CLOTHE IT. SURELY LIFE MEANS MORE THAN FOOD, AND THE BODY MORE THAN CLOTHING! (6:25) LOOK AT THE BIRDS IN THE SKY. THEY DO NOT SOW OR REAP OR GATHER INTO BARNS; YET YOUR HEAVENLY FATHER FEEDS THEM. ARE WE NOT WORTH MUCH MORE THAN THEY ARE? (6:26) CAN ANY OF YOU, FOR ALL HIS WORRYING, ADD ONE SINGLE CUBIT TO HIS SPAN OF LIFE? (6:27) AND WHY WORRY ABOUT CLOTHING? THINK OF THE FLOWERS GROWING IN THE FIELDS; THEY NEVER HAVE TO WORK or spin (6:38); yet I assure you that not even Solomon in all his regalia was robed like one of these (6:29). Now if that is how God clothes the grass in the field which is there today and thrown into the furnace tomorrow, will he not much more look after you, you men of little faith? (6:30) So do not worry; do not say, 'What are we to eat? What are we to drink? How are we to be clothed?' (6:31) It is the pagans who set their hearts on all these things. Your heavenly Father knows you need them all (6:32). Set your hearts on his kingdom first, and on his righteousness, and all these other things will be given you as well" (6:33).

Now it is fine to pray, and after you pray, leave it alone. That's trust. You trust that whatever you do sincerely in the eyes of God, whatever the outcome, it will be good for you. Trusting is to love someone enough that you trust whatever it is they do. You're willing to stand by them if they fail. God will stand by me if I fail. But constant worry, depression, anxiety, frustration, thinking "Nothing's going to change"—that is a total, total lack of trust.

It's so bad because what does it do? It keeps your mind and heart away from Jesus. And that's the whole thing. It's one of the cleverest tools of the enemy, because he makes you think you're doing right. He makes you think that you've got to solve the problem, so you have no trust that God will solve the whole thing in His time. That can have a paralyzing effect on the soul.

If you don't have trust in your life, you have little love, because trust comes from love. If you love someone deeply, you trust them. You may not understand God's ways, but you can trust that everything is going to be okay. That's what the Blessed Mother did. Just look at what she said yes to. That takes real trust. Work on trusting God, my friends, in little and big ways throughout the day. There's a beautiful book called *Abandonment to Divine Providence*—that whole book is one total act of trust. You can ask for things, but if you don't get them, keep your peace and drop it. That's trust.

Seeking God

❖

Luke 11:9–10

In the Gospel of Luke Our Lord said: "So I SAY TO YOU: ASK, AND IT WILL BE GIVEN TO YOU; SEARCH, AND YOU WILL FIND; KNOCK, AND THE DOOR WILL BE OPENED TO YOU" (11:9). And I think in here is the secret to all holiness. We need to ask, and we certainly don't have much trouble asking, do we? That is all we do. But knocking, searching, seeking, that's different. To seek someone is to look for them. The Lord promises if we look we will always find. So how do I seek the Lord: His invisible Reality, the very reason for my being, the cause of my existence? How do I reach out and say, "God, where are You and how close are You to me? How do I live with Thee?"

I think the best way to seek the Lord is to search for Him in the mundane duties of the present moment. Don't stare glumly at those egg-stained dishes that you have to scrape in the morning—see the duty of the present moment. Seek God in those dirty dishes, in that rug that you have to vacuum, in that budget that you have to balance. Seek God in the person who bugs you. Why? Because Our Dear Lord, in the Gospel of Saint John, said that if you are bearing fruit, the Father will prune you so that you may bear more fruit (Jn 15:1–8, 16).

Each one of us has a long way to go before we are perfect images of the Father. The Father loves you enough to put you in situations that you can't get away from. Are you supposed to crumble before them? Are you supposed to despair? No, in that very thing your Father, who seeks only your good and loves you with an infinite love, is pruning you. Our Father has sent this thing to make you more patient. He has sent someone to offend you so that in the act of forgiving you will "be merciful as your Father is merciful" (Lk 6:36). In the everyday, mundane things of this life, in the monotony of eating and sleeping and drinking and working—in all of this there is God, there is goodness. But you must *seek* it! If the person who tries your patience is the only thing on your mind, then you're going to be resentful and hateful. You have not sought God and you have not found God. The very thing that God permitted for your good is lost. You have not been pruned. You have become more callous and more impatient and more bitter and more unkind than ever. Seek Him in those moments, and you will find Him.

Receiving an Answer to Prayer (A Meditation)

❖

Luke 11:9–13

In our "Journey into Scripture" today, we see the Master and the apostles and they are discussing prayer. I go closer to them and listen. The Master says, "ASK, AND IT WILL BE GIVEN TO YOU; SEARCH, AND YOU WILL FIND; KNOCK, AND THE DOOR WILL BE OPENED TO YOU (11:9). FOR THE ONE WHO ASKS ALWAYS

RECEIVES; AND THE ONE WHO SEARCHES ALWAYS FINDS, THE ONE WHO KNOCKS WILL ALWAYS HAVE THE DOOR OPENED TO HIM" (11:10).

I look at the Master and say, "I am in doubt. There are many things that I have asked in your holy Name but not received. Yet You have said, 'He who asks *always* receives.' Will you explain this to me?" The Master looks up at me and says, "When you ask the Father in My Name, you must first ask for everything that is for your good. And sometimes because your sight is limited you ask for things that seem to receive no answer, as if all of heaven is closed to your prayer. In your finite mind you believe if you have this one thing, all else will be well. But the Father's one desire is to have you as close to Him in heaven, as possible. Sometimes He says no, but even in that no you have received an answer to your prayer. Your prayer should always be for the good of the kingdom and for your love.

"As a child you must have unbounded confidence in God's wisdom and know that when you pray for your good and for the good of the kingdom on earth—you always receive an answer."

I understand that now. I used to think that the answer had to be the one that I wanted. But perhaps God says no to determine how much I love Him—to bring out from the depths of my soul a love and a confidence that is so great that it will increase my glory in heaven and give courage to my neighbor. In adversity and tribulation we prove that we are disciples by holding firm.

The Master goes on and says: "When you search you always find." I ask Him, "What does it mean to seek Thee? You are invisible and I cannot touch You. When I look, I do not see You." And He says, "To seek Me is to look for Me as you would look for a friend or a loved one. To seek Me out in the daily duties of your life, to seek Me in joy and sorrow, honor and dishonor, and in everything that life gives you moment to moment—to find good and to find God; to seek Him in everything. For those who love God all things tend to good." I now realize that I have not sought God in this way. In adversity and pain and sorrow it is so hard to find Him, perhaps because I have not sought Him in these things. Then I remember that Jesus sought the Father in every occurrence in His life—in the ingratitude of the healed lepers who never said thank you, in the malice and the jealousy of those who should have loved Him.

Then the Master goes on, "WHAT FATHER AMONG YOU WOULD HAND HIS SON A STONE WHEN HE ASKED FOR BREAD? OR HAND HIM A SNAKE INSTEAD OF A FISH? (11:11). . . . IF YOU WHO ARE EVIL, KNOW HOW TO GIVE YOUR CHILDREN WHAT IS GOOD, HOW MUCH MORE WILL THE HEAVENLY FATHER GIVE THE HOLY SPIRIT TO THOSE WHO ASK HIM!" (11:13).

I suddenly realize that my concept of what is good for me and God's understanding and wisdom of what is good for me are different. I have not been a child who has trusted the Father. I have considered my wisdom superior to His, as if I know what is best for me. But I do not see tomorrow the way He sees tomorrow. I must have confidence in His wisdom and then every time I ask I shall receive, and every time I seek I shall find, and every time I knock He will come and rest in me.

Only the Violent Carry It Away

❖

Matthew 11:12

You will know in greater depth as you see the Lord's Passion and the humiliations He suffered day after day by people who didn't believe, by His own apostles—what violence He did to His purity as God. And yet He did all that violence. "THE KINGDOM OF HEAVEN HAS BEEN SUBJECTED TO VIOLENCE AND THE VIOLENT ARE TAKING IT BY STORM" (11:12). In another translation it reads ". . . only the violent carry it away." What does that mean?

It doesn't mean violence. It means I have to crush my own weaknesses to be like Jesus. I have to die to myself and that sometimes takes violence. Have you ever been on the verge of losing your temper and tried to hold it? It takes violence to do that. It's a violent thing sometimes to be meek when you want to sock somebody in the chops. It's a violent thing I do to my nature when I feel so bad and I don't want anybody around me and I'm sweet and I talk to somebody and I'm loving to them. It takes violence. When I give in to myself, I'm not being violent; I'm being careless with my own soul.

Love and Duty

❖

Luke 17:7–10

WHICH OF YOU, WITH A SERVANT PLOUGHING OR MINDING SHEEP, WOULD SAY TO HIM WHEN HE RETURNED FROM THE FIELDS, 'COME AND HAVE YOUR MEAL IMMEDIATELY'? (18:7) WOULD HE NOT BE MORE LIKELY TO SAY, 'GET MY SUPPER LAID; MAKE YOURSELF TIDY AND WAIT ON ME WHILE I EAT AND DRINK. YOU CAN EAT AND DRINK YOURSELF AFTERWARDS'? (17:8) MUST HE BE GRATEFUL TO THE SERVANT FOR DOING WHAT HE WAS TOLD? (17:9) SO WITH YOU: WHEN YOU HAVE DONE ALL YOU HAVE BEEN TOLD TO DO, SAY, 'WE ARE MERELY SERVANTS: WE HAVE DONE NO MORE THAN OUR DUTY'" (17:10).

The Lord is teaching us a very strong, hard lesson here. A thank-you is a very important thing because it shows people courtesy, that you appreciate what they're doing. But when you're talking about accomplishing a duty for God, He is not obliged to say thank you or to reward you. We can't go to heaven with any concept of an award or reward for all the exterior things we did. Those were inspirations we merely followed because it's our duty to follow the will of God. The only thing I will have when I die is the amount of love I have for God at that moment.

The Woman Caught in Adultery

❖

John 8:2–12

A T DAYBREAK HE APPEARED IN THE TEMPLE AGAIN; AND AS ALL THE PEOPLE CAME TO HIM, HE SAT DOWN AND BEGAN TO TEACH THEM (8:2). THE SCRIBES AND PHARISEES BROUGHT A WOMAN ALONG WHO HAD BEEN CAUGHT COMMITTING ADULTERY (8:3). I suppose the thing that gripes me the most is that the *guy,* who must have also been caught committing adultery, got off scot-free. But they made the woman stand in full view of everybody.

THEY SAID TO JESUS, "MASTER, THIS WOMAN WAS CAUGHT IN THE VERY ACT OF COMMITTING ADULTERY (8:4), AND MOSES HAS ORDERED US IN THE LAW TO CONDEMN WOMEN LIKE THIS TO DEATH BY STONING. WHAT HAVE YOU TO SAY?" (8:5). That was the trick of tricks really. Looks like they were setting the Lord up. (I know it doesn't say that here.) It says, THEY ASKED HIM THIS AS A TEST, LOOKING FOR SOMETHING TO USE AGAINST HIM (8:6).

The Lord was so clever. He bent down and started writing on the ground with His finger. AS THEY PERSISTED WITH THEIR QUESTION (8:7)—you get the impression that He may have been doodling in the sand. Just took His time. He may have written the accused woman's name in the dirt. And they persisted with the question, probably repeating it again: "Master, this woman was caught in adultery. The Law says we should stone her. What do You say?" It's like: "Yoo hoo, are you listening?" Then HE LOOKED UP AND SAID, "IF THERE IS ONE OF YOU

WHO HAS NOT SINNED, LET HIM BE THE FIRST TO THROW A STONE AT HER" (8:7).

Notice that He didn't say the Law should not be observed. He just said, "If all of you have not sinned (and maybe with her), then you can go ahead and punish her." She may have had a few little rendezvous with some of them. Who knows?

THEN HE BENT DOWN AND WROTE ON THE GROUND AGAIN (8:8). I imagine He was writing names, like Joseph, Simon—their names. This next bit makes you think that's exactly what He did: WHEN THEY HEARD THIS THEY WENT AWAY ONE BY ONE, BEGINNING WITH THE ELDEST, UNTIL JESUS WAS LEFT ALONE WITH THE WOMAN, WHO REMAINED STANDING THERE (8:9). She just stood there.

HE LOOKED UP AND SAID, "WOMAN, WHERE ARE THEY? HAS NO ONE CONDEMNED YOU?" (8:10). "NO ONE, SIR[,]" SHE RE-PLIED. "NEITHER DO I CONDEMN YOU," SAID JESUS[,] "GO AWAY, AND DON'T SIN ANY MORE" (8:11). What a phenomenal gift.

If we ever get discouraged over our faults and weaknesses and imperfections, if we ever even begin to get discombobu-lated because we have this fault or that fault, we should think on this moment in Jesus's life. Adultery's a pretty bad thing. But the Lord looked up and He said, "Has no one condemned you?" She said no. He said, "Well neither will I. Go and sin no more." He's very merciful and a wonderful teacher.

He forgives her but then adds that little line we often for-get: "Don't do it anymore." This is the essence of confession. Any big sin we have made a definite decision to commit, must not be repeated after absolution. Most of the things we're guilty of are little things, spur of the moment things, things that arise from our temperaments. When our temperament riles up very quickly, pride and sensitivity and all of that stuff creep in, and we fall more frequently.

WHEN JESUS SPOKE TO THE PEOPLE AGAIN, HE SAID: "I AM THE LIGHT OF THE WORLD; ANYONE WHO FOLLOWS ME WILL NOT BE WALKING IN THE DARK; HE WILL HAVE THE LIGHT OF LIFE" (8:12). I think we must look upon Jesus as our one love. Look upon Jesus as our only love, and look upon our neighbors as those whom we love because we're so in love with Jesus. When we're with Jesus, when we're in His Presence, when we're in prayer, we are in light. Anything else that occupies our mind is darkness.

He said, "I AM THE LIGHT OF THE WORLD; ANYONE WHO FOLLOWS ME"—that's an important thing: anyone who follows Him—"WILL NOT BE WALKING IN THE DARKNESS; HE WILL HAVE THE LIGHT OF LIFE" (8:12). You see, you can't give people light if you're in darkness. The only way to give light is to be *in* the light. I think it's an important passage for us to understand that if we really love Jesus, we need to live in that light. Live in the light of Jesus and everything else falls away: things, time, people, events, work—it all falls away. What is left is only the light, and that's Jesus.

Do Not Let Your Hearts Be Troubled

❖

John 14:1–2

DO NOT LET YOUR HEARTS BE TROUBLED. TRUST IN GOD STILL, AND TRUST IN ME (14:1). THERE ARE MANY ROOMS IN MY FATHER'S HOUSE; IF THERE WERE NOT, I SHOULD HAVE TOLD YOU. I AM GOING NOW TO PREPARE A PLACE FOR YOU" (14:2). "DO NOT LET YOUR HEARTS BE TROUBLED." This word is so important. Contrary to all the things that go wrong in our lives, the things that don't come up to par, the things I expected that failed to materialize—in spite of all that, or perhaps because of it, we must trust in the Lord, trust in God. The reason we allow our hearts to be troubled is that we don't trust. Why else would you be troubled? There's no reason to be troubled if you trust the Lord.

Jesus goes on to give us a reason for not allowing our hearts to be troubled. He says, "THERE ARE MANY ROOMS IN MY FATHER'S HOUSE." We must realize that we have something coming that's much greater than what I'm troubled about having or not having, or what I would like or not like, or whether things go my way or not. Our hearts are always troubled, my friends, always troubled when we don't get what we want or expect. Our Lord is saying, "Look to the future."

The Father has many, many rooms in His house, and He's going to prepare a place for me. Think about that. God is preparing that place through all of your joys, sorrows, health, sickness—everything in your life is of value to God, and He uses everything. He never wastes a thing, not even your faults and weaknesses. He makes you want to repent, and even though you rebel against the present moment, He said, "I AM GOING NOW TO PREPARE A PLACE FOR YOU." Shouldn't that take the place of anything you're disappointed in? I have been chosen by God, and He is, at this moment, preparing a place for me. What a reassurance that is.

The Grace of the Word

When we talk about the Word of God, we are talking about Jesus. The Word of the Father is Jesus.

The Word of God is something very awesome and precious. Any book you read can be beautiful and inspiring, it can be searing—meaning it can really convict you—but in no way is it like the Word, because the Word of God pierces the heart, and when it enters the soul it brings with it grace. That is not true of any other book.

If you read this one sentence that I just opened up to— "Do not let your hearts be troubled"—even *reading* the Word brings grace to your heart.

In the Eastern Church they kneel, they genuflect before the Word. And I think we need to renew our love for the Word and recognize that the Word brings grace.

Read your books of the world, but absorb the Word, without which we cannot grow in His image. If I don't know Him, I can't grow in Him. What makes me like Him the most is taking this Word and placing it in my heart and soul, and that is what will make you, and your life, beautiful.

Shake the Dust

❖

Luke 10:5–10, 12

WHATEVER HOUSE YOU GO INTO, LET YOUR FIRST WORDS BE, 'PEACE TO THIS HOUSE!' (10:5). AND IF A MAN OF PEACE LIVES THERE, YOUR PEACE WILL GO AND REST ON HIM; IF NOT, IT WILL COME BACK TO YOU" (10:6). Our problem is we lose our peace if we're not accepted the way we want to be accepted. We're not able to let people go and move on. You know? Our Lord is very clear: You offered peace, they didn't take your peace, let it go.

"STAY IN THE SAME HOUSE, TAKING WHAT FOOD AND DRINK THEY HAVE TO OFFER, FOR THE LABOURER DESERVES HIS WAGES; DO NOT MOVE FROM HOUSE TO HOUSE (10.7). WHENEVER YOU GO INTO A TOWN WHERE THEY MAKE YOU WELCOME, EAT WHAT IS SET BEFORE YOU" (10:8). (So don't be a fussbudget.) "CURE THOSE IN IT WHO ARE SICK, AND SAY, 'THE KINGDOM OF GOD IS VERY NEAR TO YOU' (10:0). BUT WHENEVER YOU ENTER A TOWN AND THEY DO NOT MAKE YOU WELCOME, GO OUT INTO ITS STREETS AND SAY (10:10), 'WE WIPE OFF THE VERY DUST OF YOUR TOWN THAT CLINGS TO OUR FEET, AND LEAVE IT WITH YOU'" (10:11). Our Lord was not interested in the hygiene of your tootsies. He is saying if you're trying to talk to someone and they won't listen to you, don't bring that heartache along with you the rest of the day. Shake it off! If you're not accepted, if what you say is not accepted, whether they like you or they don't—don't permit that dust (He calls it dust), don't permit that incident, that occasion, that person to reside in your house for the rest of the day, the rest of the month, the rest of the year.

If we understood that one principle we'd be saints by tomorrow morning at nine-thirty. Because it isn't the present moment that gripes you, it's what happened two days ago that lingers in your mind and heart. You don't shake it. It goes around like a three-act play, and then it's a four-act play, and then it's a five-act play, and the first thing you know, you've created a drama over nothing. And the Lord said, "Shake it! Wipe off the very dust of it!"

Our Lord is teaching us that if you offer peace and people don't accept it, don't let it bother you. Keep your peace, and shake their dust from your feet.

The Lord pronounces a warning here: "I TELL YOU, ON THAT DAY IT WILL NOT GO AS HARD WITH SODOM AS WITH THAT TOWN" (10:12). That's pretty heavy stuff. The apostle who came there to preach the Gospel wasn't accepted—and there is a price to pay for that rejection.

I think that's a good lesson for us in our daily life when we think we ought to be affecting somebody and we're not. We ought to just shake the dust from our feet! We just have to let it go, and leave it to God. We would like to think we're the ones who are going to convert everybody, but others will follow, other events will follow, other circumstances will follow, and God will take care of them there. That's where prayer is so important. If I pray much, I may not see the fruit of my prayer, I may not see it in this life, but prayer is powerful—and because it's powerful, it never dies.

The Parable of the Two Sons
(A Meditation)

❖

Matthew 21:28–31

During our spiritual journey, we see the Master speaking to a crowd of people. He has been asked by some of the Pharisees by what authority He teaches and acts as He does. He looks out at the crowd and says, "WHAT IS YOUR OPINION? A MAN HAD TWO SONS. HE WENT AND SAID TO THE FIRST, 'MY BOY, YOU GO AND WORK IN THE VINEYARD TODAY' (21:28). HE ANSWERED, 'I WILL NOT GO,' BUT AFTERWARDS THOUGHT BETTER OF IT AND WENT (21:29). THE MAN THEN WENT AND SAID THE SAME THING TO THE SECOND WHO ANSWERED, 'CERTAINLY, SIR,' BUT DID NOT GO" (21:30).

The Lord looks out at the crowd and asks: "WHICH OF THE TWO DID THE FATHER'S WILL?" "THE FIRST," THEY SAID (21:31).

I look at the Master and joy wells up in my heart because I see myself in the first son. How many times has the Lord asked me to do things, some easy and some hard? I have said no, and I have rebelled and then thought it over, and went out and did it. If only I had gone out and done the Lord's will the first time with joy. If only I had not gotten angry and rebelled. And I look at the Master and He looks at me and says, "Fear not. It is the accomplishment of His will that shows love, not how you do it. Sometimes it is difficult and poor human nature rebels, but love conquers all." Then I realize that love demands sacrifice. I went out and did the Father's will even when it was hard.

And He was pleased. If I continue this, I will soon adopt a habit of doing the Father's will and more easily see the Father's love, not just a command. Sometimes that love requires the sacrifice of something in this world, but the Father will make it up to you.

I make a vow never to hesitate before a request of the Lord, but to always say yes and to fulfill it with great haste.

I Am the Vine, You Are the Branches

❖

John 15:5–6

I AM THE VINE, YOU ARE THE BRANCHES. WHOEVER REMAINS IN ME, WITH ME IN HIM, BEARS FRUIT IN PLENTY; FOR CUT OFF FROM ME YOU CAN DO NOTHING (15:5). ANYONE WHO DOES NOT REMAIN IN ME IS LIKE A BRANCH THAT HAS BEEN THROWN AWAY—HE WITHERS; THESE BRANCHES ARE COLLECTED AND THROWN ON THE FIRE, AND THEY ARE BURNT" (15:6).

What's so marvelous about Jesus is His awesome humility. He calls Himself the vine, which means that unless we're *in* Jesus we become a kind of wild plant. Then the enemy comes and just pushes you back and forth in your heart, your mind, your soul and everything spirals out of control. Without the vine—the root—the branches wither. But the Lord said that His Father is the vinedresser and prunes the branches. Some say, "I don't want to be pruned. I'm strong and I want to go my own way." Well, that "branch" will grow. But the older it gets and the faster it grows, the less value it will have. It is of no use. It begins to wither—it overgrows itself. It self-destructs in time. Unruly vines bear thistles; they don't bear fruit. Sometimes that's the deception in our lives. We think we are growing, we're doing this, we're doing that, but if we don't bear fruit and if we don't allow the Lord to prune us, it may all be for naught.

The fruit of our life is found in a deep union with Jesus. We have to never forget our real vocation. Our real vocation is not the things the Lord asks us to do but to be attentive to the will of God as it manifests itself in the present moment.

God's will is frustrated many, many times, usually when we're not clinging to the Lord. We just don't cling to the Lord in our hearts, minds, and souls. Look at the Gospel: You have Matthew who was not one that Peter wanted around at all. I mean, we're talking about a tax collector who was a thief, a rabble-rouser; he was a traitor who left the synagogue. He left his faith and became a tax collector, and he collected from his own people! Well, here comes Jesus and He says, "Follow me" (Mt 9:9). I bet you some of those apostles, especially Simon the Zealot, must have had a fit. You see, God's ways are not our ways, and He picked a sinner to bear fruit on His vine. But Matthew, and Magdalene, and Thomas (who was a doubter), and Peter (who was a hothead), and John, and all of them, with all their faults and weaknesses, clung to Jesus. And when they clung to Jesus, they bore fruit. So I think in our own lives we need to examine ourselves once in a while and say, "Am I bearing fruit?" If I'm not, it's only because I'm not clinging to Jesus.

Let's ask the Lord, as the Spirit, to make us fruitful branches on His vine, on His Son's vine. Let us ask the Spirit to increase within us a great thirst for God, a great thirst for holiness. Let us ask Him to make us so holy, and so in love with our Bridegroom, that it will be a foretaste of heaven. Whether we have the pains of the martyrs or the dryness of the great mystics; whether we have health, sickness, or death—may we still love Jesus all the days of our lives.

The Kingdom

❖

Matthew 16:28; 3:2

The Lord says, "I TELL YOU SOLEMNLY, THERE ARE SOME OF THESE STANDING HERE WHO WILL NOT TASTE DEATH BE- FORE THEY SEE THE SON OF MAN COMING WITH HIS KINGDOM" (16:28). What does that mean?

It refers to the resurrection. That was the Kingdom. Re- demption began at the incarnation, but the opening of the Kingdom began at the resurrection and the ascension. Some of those listening to the Lord would see the resurrection. A bit earlier John the Baptist announced, "[T]HE KINGDOM OF HEAVEN IS CLOSE AT HAND" (3:2). What he is saying is: at this point in time there are no more promises. The promise is ful- filled in the Messiah. So the Kingdom of heaven is at hand. Here it is. The Messiah is here, and now there is an oppor- tunity for you to be a son of God by baptism, to be an heir to the Kingdom by baptism. Without this opportunity you and I would be nothing.

Bearing Fruit (A Meditation)

❖

Matthew 7:15–20

It is the cool of the night, and the Lord is sitting in a semi-circle with the apostles, and one of them asks: "How do you know a real prophet? They all look good and sound so good. How do you know which is from God?" The Lord says to them, "You must beware of false prophets and those who come to you disguised as sheep and underneath are wolves."

Peter looks at the Master and says, "That's the point. How do you know?" And the Master says, "You will be able to tell them by their fruits. Can people pick grapes from thorns, or figs from thistles? (7:16) In the same way, a sound tree produces good fruit but a rotten tree bad fruit" (7:17).

I catch the Master's eye and I say, "What do you mean by fruit?" He says, "You will know if someone is living the life of a child of God by his conduct." And I say to Him, "You just said false prophets look like sheep but are wolves on the inside." He said, "Yes, their actions are good but their fruit are bad. When a Christian loves his neighbor in the same way God loves him (as he is); when a Christian is patient with the faults of others; when he realizes that sanctity of life takes time and that each fall demands rising to greater heights; when a Christian has joy of heart and can accept anything that life gives him with serenity of soul; when he has unbounded confidence in His Father's love for him—this is bearing fruit. A man and a woman will be known by their fruit. A pagan must see the

Father in you so that he can believe that the Father sent Me and I sent you."

I begin to understand that it means more to *be* a Christian than to be called a Christian. It means that God in me must grow brighter and brighter and as the image of Jesus grows in my soul, I must bear fruit.

The Lord then says something that chills me: "ANY TREE THAT DOES NOT PRODUCE GOOD FRUIT IS CUT DOWN AND THROWN ON THE FIRE (7:19). I REPEAT, YOU WILL BE ABLE TO TELL THEM BY THEIR FRUITS" (7:20).

SAINTLY CONTEMPLATION

Learn to abide with attention in loving, waiting upon God in the state of quiet. Contemplation is nothing else but a secret, peaceful and loving infusion of God, which, if admitted, will set the soul on fire with the Spirit of love.

— SAINT JOHN OF THE CROSS

The Eucharist

❖

John 6:53–69

Whenever Our Dear Lord says, "I TELL YOU SOLEMNLY" (6:53), that means you should listen very closely. So perk up your ears. "[I]F YOU DO NOT EAT THE FLESH OF THE SON OF MAN AND DRINK HIS BLOOD, YOU WILL NOT HAVE LIFE IN YOU (6:53). ANYONE WHO DOES EAT MY FLESH AND DRINK MY BLOOD HAS ETERNAL LIFE, AND I SHALL RAISE HIM UP ON THE LAST DAY" (6:54). This is very, very deep doctrine and Jesus does not dilute it—He doesn't tone it down at all. When He speaks of the vine and branches in John, it is obvious that this is a symbol of our relationship with Him. He didn't say unless you eat my vine you shall not have life in you. Everybody understood that it was a symbol.

But here He is talking about something that if it *were* true would be very, very disconcerting to these people because they had no context to place it in. When He said, "IF YOU DO NOT EAT THE FLESH OF THE SON OF MAN AND DRINK HIS BLOOD, YOU WILL NOT HAVE LIFE IN YOU," the only thing they can think of is the old sacrifices and cannibalism. That's what cannibals do; they eat you up, literally. What a shocking doctrine, and yet He goes on as if it were the most common thing in the world.

"FOR MY FLESH IS REAL FOOD AND MY BLOOD IS REAL DRINK (6:55). HE WHO EATS MY FLESH AND DRINKS MY BLOOD"—again, this is a repetition; He just got through saying it—"LIVES IN ME AND I LIVE IN HIM" (6:56). He is speaking of Holy Communion, the Body and Blood of Christ. It is unbelievable that God would think of such a thing. If we thought of it, it would be blasphemy. The very idea that God would make Himself bread and wine and then be our food—it is unbelievable. But when the Son of God says it, it is *unbelievable* love and *unbelievable* humility. Think about what He has done. He goes wherever you want Him to go. He's there all day long in many churches throughout the world. And too often every door is locked. God is locked away from His people. They say they're afraid of robbers. Well, put an alarm in there or pay a guard, but don't shut the people away from the Lord. What a horrible thing to do.

"As I, who am sent by the living Father, myself draw life from the Father, so whoever eats me will draw life from me" (6:57). This means that He is the living image of the Father. When Philip said, "Lord, let us see the Father and then we shall be satisfied" (14:8), I would have slapped him down, but the Lord said, "To have seen me is to have seen . . ." Who? "The Father" (14:9). Why? Because Jesus is the perfect image of the Father's knowledge of Himself. So he who sees Jesus sees the Father. That's why when you look at the Host you see the Father, Son, and Holy Ghost.

"This is the bread come down from heaven; not like the bread our ancestors ate: they are dead, but anyone who eats this bread will live forever" (6:58). He taught this doctrine at Capernaum—very important—in the synagogue (6:59). This is one of the few times where the word "doctrine" is uttered in Scripture.

After hearing it, many of his followers—now, you know, it doesn't say just the Pharisees but His *followers*—said, "This is intolerable language. How could anyone accept it?" (6:60). They just can't accept it. "This is for the birds," they are saying. It's still that way today: Many consider this intolerable language. Even the Fundamentalists, who take the

Scripture at face value, say, "This is ridiculous." They take this whole chapter and throw it out the window. They never mention it.

This is a point you have to understand: If Jesus did not mean what He said, then He was obliged in justice to explain it.

JESUS WAS AWARE — this is a very important passage, Jesus was *aware* — THAT HIS FOLLOWERS WERE COMPLAINING (6:61). If He was only speaking symbolically, then Jesus, because He was Infinite Justice, was obliged to explain to everybody, "This is a symbol." But instead He says, "DOES THIS UPSET YOU?" (6:61). Oh, Jesus was so strong. He could care less about human respect. "WHAT IF YOU SHOULD SEE THE SON OF MAN ASCEND TO WHERE HE WAS BEFORE?" (6:62).

He's saying: "If this upsets you, how are you going to accept Jesus, Me, as Son of God defying death?" That's what He was saying. "How are you going to accept that I will ascend to the right hand of the Father if you can't accept this?" "IT IS THE SPIRIT THAT GIVES LIFE, THE FLESH HAS NOTHING TO OFFER. THE WORDS I HAVE SPOKEN TO YOU ARE SPIRIT AND THEY ARE LIFE" (6:63). What does the priest say before the consecration? He puts his hand over the host and he says, "By the power of Thy Spirit may this become the Body and Blood, Soul and Divinity of Your Son, Jesus Christ." That's the whole essence of Catholicism.

"BUT THERE ARE SOME OF YOU WHO DO NOT BELIEVE." FOR JESUS KNEW FROM THE OUTSET THOSE WHO DID NOT BELIEVE, AND WHO IT WAS THAT WOULD BETRAY HIM (6:64). Now, most of us would be terribly crushed if some of our faithful friends had turned around and walked away. Crushed to pieces. One of the most crushing blows in life would be to have dear friends walk away. He looks at them walking away and says, "THIS IS WHY I TOLD YOU NO ONE COULD COME TO ME UNLESS THE FATHER

ALLOWS HIM" (6:65). AFTER THIS, MANY OF HIS DISCIPLES—it doesn't say Pharisees; it doesn't say Sadducees; it doesn't say scribes; it says *disciples*—STOPPED GOING WITH HIM (6:66). They went back to the synagogue, back to their old ways. This Man didn't say what they wanted Him to say.

It's an amazing chapter. You ought to read it yourself today and try to mull it over. Find out what the Lord is saying to you there. See, His disciples stopped going with Him—but isn't that true today? How many priests, how many Sisters, how many laity have stopped following the Lord because they no longer believe in the Eucharist? They don't have the guts to stand up and be counted.

The spirit of the Gospel is to love in the same way God loves me, which is most difficult because I cannot love you in the same way God loves me unless I understand the Eucharist. The Eucharist is self-sacrificing, the Eucharist is obedient, the Eucharist is dependent. He's dependent on the priest, dependent on the people for attention and love. You put Him in the tabernacle, He stays there. If someone tramples Him on the ground, He says nothing. When He goes into sacrilegious hearts, He remains silent. He is totally given to His neighbor—totally given. Which means that if I am to love my neighbor as God loves me, I must be totally given. I do not have to feel anything—I must simply give of myself to my neighbor. I must be dependent; I must not be afraid to be dependent on others. Why? Because the love of God is totally dependent. He's humble.

Another way to love my neighbor is to be self-sacrificing like the Eucharist. In other words, I prefer the good of my neighbor to myself. If I can do those things for my neighbor, I can rest assured that I love my neighbor in the same way God loves me.

Now, all of His disciples, many of them, have left. In fact, it looks like they all left Him at this point because it says here that JESUS SAID TO THE TWELVE, "WHAT ABOUT YOU, DO YOU WANT TO GO AWAY TOO?" (6:67). Now, here's Jesus willing to sacrifice even the apostles for the sake of this truth—Jesus, the Eucharist, is the Truth. It is His Body, His Blood, His Soul, His Divinity. He lost most of His disciples. He lost a lot of them there. Now He's looking at the Twelve and He's saying, "You want to go away, too? Are you going?" And Peter said, "LORD, WHO SHALL WE GO TO? YOU HAVE THE MESSAGE OF ETER-NAL LIFE (6:68), AND WE BELIEVE; WE KNOW THAT YOU ARE THE HOLY ONE OF GOD" (6:69). So here's Peter saying he doesn't understand it, but he believes. That's what faith is all about.

When you try to understand the Scripture, your faith will be in jeopardy because you cannot understand it. You can get inspiration from it, the Lord will give you some light, but to say you understand—Peter didn't understand any more than did the people who walked away, but he believed, and we must believe as well.

Joy in the Lord
❖
John 16:21–22

Our Lord said: "A WOMAN IN CHILDBIRTH SUFFERS, BE-CAUSE HER TIME HAS COME; BUT WHEN SHE HAS GIVEN BIRTH TO THE CHILD SHE FORGETS THE SUFFERING IN HER JOY THAT A MAN HAS BEEN BORN INTO THE WORLD (16:21). SO IT IS WITH YOU: YOU ARE SAD NOW, BUT I SHALL SEE YOU AGAIN, AND

YOUR HEARTS WILL BE FULL OF JOY, AND THAT JOY NO ONE SHALL TAKE FROM YOU" (16:22).

The kind of joy that Our Lord is talking about is the serenity of soul that comes from being satisfied with what God is doing in your life, not what YOU are doing in your life.

Look, you can always do better, but to be satisfied with what God is doing in your life, that brings joy. It's a joy that brings a serene acceptance of God's will in the present moment.

Happiness is a spurt of satisfaction, and those feelings come and go very quickly. But joy is different. That's why our Lord said here, "[Y]OUR HEARTS WILL BE FULL OF JOY, AND THAT JOY NO ONE SHALL TAKE FROM YOU."

So the joy we have is in what? The resurrection. The resurrection gives us joy not only because it proves that Jesus is the Lord, but because we too shall be resurrected one day and the difficulties of the moment are all going to pass.

From the Rock to Satan

❖

Matthew 16:16–23

Peter, the great blunderer, the one who always spoke before he thought (you probably know twenty people like that) one day said, "YOU ARE THE CHRIST" (16:16). AND THE LORD SAID TO HIM, "YOU ARE PETER AND ON THIS ROCK I WILL BUILD MY CHURCH (16:18). . . . I WILL GIVE YOU THE KEYS OF THE KINGDOM OF HEAVEN" (16:19). Then what happened?

The Lord starts to tell Peter about His going into Jerusalem to die. Peter takes the Lord aside and says, "[T]HIS MUST NOT HAPPEN TO YOU." LORD, DON'T GO! (16:22). Now if you know the Lord is going to die if He goes to Jerusalem, isn't it logical to ask Him not to go? Wouldn't you say the same thing?

The Lord makes Peter the rock, the foundation of His Church, five minutes before, and now He looks at him and says, "GET BEHIND ME, SATAN" (16:23). Oh what a comedown: the leader one moment and the devil the next. Isn't that your life? Don't you feel so good one moment and like the devil the next? Peter was trying to stop the Lord from completing His mission, and that He could not allow.

But God held onto Peter, kept him as an apostle—and He keeps us too. Because you're human you're going to rise and fall. Scripture says somewhere that "THE VIRTUOUS MAN FALLS SEVEN TIMES" (Prv 24:16). For most of us that would be a good day. So don't lose courage because you fall. You don't need anything else in this life except to become holy and to remain close to God. And don't fail to make the distinction between the rejection of God and imperfections. There's a big difference between the two.

Love Your Enemies

❖

Matthew 5:43–45

In Saint Matthew's Gospel, we find some prerogatives of the Father, given to us so that we might imitate God. Most of the hallmarks of the Father, the attributes of the Father, are beyond us. But here is one we can accomplish: "YOU HAVE LEARNT HOW IT WAS SAID: YOU MUST LOVE YOUR NEIGHBOUR AND HATE

YOUR ENEMY (5:43). BUT I SAY THIS TO YOU: LOVE YOUR ENEMIES AND PRAY FOR THOSE WHO PERSECUTE YOU" (5:44). I must love my enemy as the Father loves His enemies. The Father does good to His enemies and so I must pray for mine, and "IN THIS WAY YOU WILL BE SONS OF YOUR FATHER IN HEAVEN" (5:45).

Then He says: "FOR HE CAUSES HIS SUN TO RISE ON BAD MEN AS WELL AS GOOD, AND HIS RAIN TO FALL ON HONEST AND DISHONEST MEN ALIKE" (5:45). In the Lord's mind there can be no difference between a person who is holy, a person who is faulty, a person who is a big sinner, or a person who is pious. There's no difference. Jesus in His love always said He hated sin—hated sin—but He loved the sinner. We seldom separate the sin from the sinner. So, if I hate your way of life, I hate you. If I despise your faults, I despise you.

Love has a way of minimizing faults. They've got these minimizing bras—what do they do? They're supposed to make something big look like something small. Well, that's what our love should do. Love minimizes the faults of others.

I used to have a superior, and I hated going to spiritual direction with her because when I'd share all my gripes, she'd say, "Well, you have to cover it over with a mantle of charity." I used to just about die. It was the same line every month. I'd never say anything, but I thought, "God, if I hear that one more time . . ." But she was right. See, my solution to every problem was to wipe it out: if you can't change them, get rid of them. My solution seemed a lot simpler than hers; but her solution was right. When I started loving this one particular individual, her faults were still there, but I found it easier to overlook them. It worked for me. The compassion I began to feel for this individual, through loving, overcame my bitterness; it didn't change her in any way, but it overcame my bitterness over what she was or was not doing.

So the first thing we must do is love everybody. In that way we can be perfect as the Father in heaven is perfect. Perfection consists of totally accepting every individual, with all of their weaknesses, their foibles, and loving them exactly as they are.

Advice for Praying

❖

Matthew 6:7–8

The Lord gives you some tips on prayer. He says, "IN YOUR PRAYERS DO NOT BABBLE AS THE PAGANS DO, FOR THEY THINK THAT BY USING MANY WORDS THEY WILL MAKE THEMSELVES HEARD (6:7). DO NOT BE LIKE THEM; YOUR FATHER KNOWS WHAT YOU NEED BEFORE YOU ASK HIM" (6:8). The logical follow-up to this is: Why are you asking at all? If the Father knows what you need, and will provide it, why do you have to ask?

Well, it is God's will that you ask because it gives Him greater joy. Secondly, He wants to build a desire in our hearts to possess what is good and holy. He then wants to fulfill that desire. Making a request of God also gives you a deep awareness of His immediate response to you—His loving concern for you. The Father-daughter/Father-son relationship is built upon asking, that you may receive.

Think about it: Don't you want somebody you love to ask for something? So often surprise gifts are not what the other person really wants. You learn that at Christmas. How many men get umpteen neckties at Christmas because you don't know what else to give them? The immediacy with which something is given (or sometimes refused) is always indicative of the love of the beloved—which means that God Who is

Father wants to act like a father. He just doesn't want to pour stuff into your lap. The asking is so you can appreciate His generosity. What the Lord is saying here is don't *worry* about the things you need. But He still wants you to ask and He wants to fulfill your needs.

The Plank in Your Eye

❖

Luke 6:41–45

Our Lord said, "WHY DO YOU OBSERVE THE SPLINTER IN YOUR BROTHER'S EYE AND NEVER NOTICE THE PLANK IN YOUR OWN? (6:41) HOW CAN YOU SAY TO YOUR BROTHER, 'BROTHER, LET ME TAKE OUT THE SPLINTER THAT IS IN YOUR EYE' WHEN YOU CANNOT SEE THE PLANK IN YOUR OWN?" (6:42).

Our Dear Lord calls all the faults we find in others "a splinter." And knowing us as He does, He says, "You've got an awful lot to account for. Why are you looking at that splinter?" The Lord calls us "hypocrites" (6:42). I think that's funny. That was His favorite word: "hypocrite." He uses it an awful lot.

"TAKE THE PLANK OUT OF YOUR OWN EYE FIRST, AND THEN YOU WILL SEE CLEARLY ENOUGH TO TAKE OUT THE SPLINTER THAT IS IN YOUR BROTHER'S EYE" (6:42).

He's not saying there's not a splinter in your brother's eye. What He's saying is unless you overcome yourself, you can't help somebody else overcome themselves. You haven't gone through the process. Now, just imagine if you took that as a model for your life. Just imagine what would happen to you. You would be so conscious of your own sinner condition that it would never dawn on you that anybody else did anything wrong. Why? Because whatever they do, regardless of what you think, the Lord God calls it a splinter.

Now why does He do that? Because when I offend God, it's a plank, it's a big thing. If my neighbor offends me, it's a very little thing. That's what He's saying. So why can't you forgive little things when God has forgiven some pretty big planks in your life? That's the whole point.

He keeps saying, "If you took that plank out of your own eye, you would see clearly. You would see the difference between your brother's fault and your own. Then you would not be as critical, but more charitable. That would help you love a lot more."

Our Lord always used little things. He transformed bread and wine into His Body and Blood. He said if you give a cup of cold water to one in need you get an eternal reward. If you feed the poor you get a great reward. And so, in our lifetime, in our daily life, you have to look past the big things, to the little things. He even said, "[U]NLESS YOU CHANGE AND BECOME LIKE LITTLE CHILDREN YOU WILL NEVER ENTER THE KINGDOM OF HEAVEN" (Mt 18:3). That's an awesome remark because it says if you're not little in your heart, if you're not humble, trusting, forgiving, and generous with love, you will not see heaven.

Littleness. That's why some people have a hard time being humble, because they can't be little. They cannot be aware of their nothingness without becoming disheartened and discouraged. But littleness of heart is so important.

Let's always remember to take the planks out of our own eyes, and look to little things, understanding that little things make us great, and little things make us extremely imperfect.

Rooted to God's Will
(A Meditation)

❖

Mark 4:3–20

We are in Jerusalem, and the Master is with a great crowd of people, and He tells them: "The kingdom of heaven is like a sower who goes out to sow his seed." I can imagine a farmer going out and sowing seed. Jesus says, "Now it happened that, as he sowed, some of the seed fell on the edge of the path, and the birds came and ate it up (4:4). Some seed fell on rocky ground where it found little soil and sprang up straightaway, because there was no depth of earth (4:5); and when the sun came up it was scorched and, not having any roots, it withered away (4:6). Some seed fell into thorns, and the thorns grew up and choked it, and it produced no crop (4:7). And some seeds fell into rich soil and, growing tall and strong, produced crop; and yielded thirty, sixty, even a hundredfold" (4:8). And he said, "Listen anyone who has ears to hear!" (4:9).

Later, I listen as Peter asks the Lord to explain the parable of the sower and the seed. The Master gently says to Peter, "What the sower is sowing is the word (4:14). Those on the edge of the path where the word is sown are people who have no sooner heard it than Satan comes and carries away the word that was sown in them (4:15). Similarly, those who receive the seed on patches of rock are people who,

WHEN FIRST THEY HEAR THE WORD, WELCOME IT AT ONCE WITH JOY (4:16). BUT THEY HAVE NO ROOT IN THEM, THEY DO NOT LAST; SHOULD SOME TRIAL COME, OR SOME PERSECUTION ON ACCOUNT OF THE WORD, THEY FALL AWAY AT ONCE (4:17). THEN THERE ARE OTHERS WHO RECEIVE THE SEED IN THORNS. THESE HAVE HEARD THE WORD (4:18), BUT THE WORRIES OF THIS WORLD, THE LURE OF RICHES AND ALL THE OTHER PASSIONS COME IN TO CHOKE THE WORD, AND SO IT PRODUCES NOTHING (4:19). AND THERE ARE THOSE WHO HAVE RECEIVED THE SEED IN RICH SOIL: THEY HEAR THE WORD AND ACCEPT IT AND YIELD A HARVEST, THIRTY AND SIXTY AND A HUNDREDFOLD" (4:20).

It's wonderful to know God's love for me, and that there is a kingdom hereafter, but what kind of root does it have within me?

For some the Word does not last—because the moment some trial comes along, some tragedy, some pain, they lose faith and their joy is gone. They begin to think there is no God. Or perhaps a persecution comes because they did believe, and the faith is completely lost—they fall away. Then there are those who receive the Word, but the lures of the world, the lures of riches, choke the Word—pleasure, the easy way out. These are the people for whom the seed fell on thorny ground. They don't want God; they want only the things of this world. They can't possess anything without being attached to it. And so they lose out, choked by the pleasures and the cares of this world. Then there are those who receive the Word. Their hearts are rich with love, and these, each one, harvests different kinds of fruit. The harvest is different. Some yield a hundredfold and they give and give and give, and when the storm comes their roots go deeper and they withstand the storm and they grow strong like a tree does. It bends with the storm but never cracks.

I look at the Master and say, "How can I bear a hundred-fold?"

He says, "By doing the Father's will with love and with joy." *

But I find doing the Father's will so difficult. It isn't as if the Father comes down and tells me what to do. "What is God's will?" I ask.

He says, "In any given situation you do what you think the Father wants you to do. Be guided by the light that you have in the present moment and the Father will stand by you—He understands. Find God and God's will in the duties of the present moment."

"Do you mean every duty?" I ask the Master.

"Yes," He says. "Perform the duty of the present moment with great love and affection and receive whatever the Father sends you moment to moment with great love and you will find God and bear fruit a hundredfold."

Necessary Reading

It's very necessary, if you want to grow in holiness, to read the Scriptures and other spiritual books. To discover how men and women who had the courage and strength to live the Gospel lived. You need that food, that nourishment, that example. You've got to ask for faith every day and immerse yourself in the experience of those people who exercised their faith. You have to read the Scriptures. You've got to do it, and then act on what you've read.

Up a Tree with Zaccheus

✦

Luke 19:1–10

Chapter 19 of Luke gives us a glimpse into the virtue of being childlike, the virtue of having no human respect, the virtue of repentance and generosity and great desire. So you have four entirely different virtues that are depicted in this small paragraph of Scripture, and all of these virtues were possessed, quite suddenly, by a sinner. We would all like to possess these virtues—and this man, Zaccheus seemingly attained them by doing one act. One act. This Gospel proves just how generous the Lord is over one act.

Now, [Jesus] entered Jericho and was going through the town (19:1) when a man whose name was Zaccheus made his appearance; he was one of the senior tax collectors and a wealthy man (19:2). Here's a man who was a publican, a senior publican, which meant he was head of all the other publicans. They were kind of the first-century Internal Revenue Service, except they were thieves. They were really the Jewish mafia. So the tax was 10 percent for Rome and 15 percent for Zaccheus. Anyway, that's why they were hated by the Jews. They were in league with Rome, and collected Roman taxes. And if you weren't nice to them, they'd pile another 5 percent on your bill. Needless to say, they were not accepted in the synagogue. But they could care less, they were making a bundle. You've got to keep all of that in mind when we look at this Zaccheus.

He was anxious to see what kind of man Jesus was

(19:3). He's curious, nosy. The Lord is using even his faults. It's an amazing thing about God: He uses even our faults, our weaknesses, and our imperfections. Zacchaeus probably heard about this man and said, "I wonder what he's like. I'm going to have a peek."

BUT HE WAS TOO SHORT AND COULD NOT SEE HIM FOR THE CROWD (19:3). Zacchaeus was very short—maybe five feet, maybe four foot eleven, who knows—and that would have only made him more hated, because they would have considered him half a man. And you can see the thieving qualities in this guy: he's ingenious, he's undaunted, he's looking for an angle. So he decides to run ahead.

You can just visualize this little guy racing ahead desperate for some way to see over the crowd. In the moment, he decides to climb a sycamore tree. He is determined to catch a glimpse of this Man, that's all he wants. He's just curious, waiting in a tree to see Jesus.

It shows us something, doesn't it? It shows us that sometimes when we're up a tree, it's a pretty good place to be. Many times we're up a tree in our spiritual lives. Maybe we can't see beyond our pettiness and faults. We can't see beyond the pettiness of other people or their cruelty. All of this towers above us and we can feel very short. You ever feel that way? But we've got to rise above all of that spiritually and look beyond people, beyond ourselves, beyond things, to Jesus. That's what Zacchaeus did. He rose above it all to search for the Lord. What he couldn't do by stature he did by climbing a tree.

SO HE RAN AHEAD AND CLIMBED A SYCAMORE TREE TO CATCH A GLIMPSE OF JESUS WHO WAS TO PASS THAT WAY (19:4). WHEN JESUS REACHED THE SPOT HE LOOKED UP (19:5). To me it's a very exciting incident. Here's this guy up in this tree and he's looking around. When he sees the Lord he's probably thinking,

"Boy, He's so tall!" Then the Lord looks right at him, with the most perfect, gentle, beautiful eyes and He calls this man by name. He didn't say, "Hey there, who are you?" He says, "ZAC-CHAEUS, COME DOWN. HURRY" (19:5). Unbelievable. This old sinner. "HURRY, BECAUSE I MUST STAY AT YOUR HOUSE TODAY" (19:5). The Lord didn't just invite Himself over; He is basically saying, "Your house is going to be mine today." And you can almost feel that little heart of Zacchaeus beating like it was coming out of his chest.

AND HE HURRIED DOWN—I imagine him shimmying all the way down to the street—AND WELCOMED HIM JOYFULLY (19:6).

Here's a man who knows he's a sinner: he's ostracized by the people, he's a thief, he's got a lot of money that doesn't do him much good, and along comes the Master: the one they call Messiah. He says, "HURRY. COME DOWN, BECAUSE I MUST STAY AT YOUR HOUSE TODAY." Wouldn't it be great if every sinner knew that all it took was a little desire on their part, and the Lord would come and stay with them? Not only that, but He wants them to "hurry."

You know, the compassion of Jesus at this point is so astronomical, but we just can't imagine Jesus desiring us because we think our weaknesses and imperfections stand in the way. The Lord sees beyond all that. When it comes to the heart, Jesus sees all, and He saw the heart of Zacchaeus—that's all He saw. I think what hurts Him the most in us is not our sins or our weaknesses but that we concentrate on them too much. We obsess over them. We're so attuned to our failings and on being perfect that we forget about Jesus.

What happened to Zacchaeus? Well, the people start grumbling. Here's the most hated man in the city and the Lord invites Himself to dinner and for a stay at his house! That means that all the people who wanted to see Jesus had to go to Zacchaeus's house.

When He said He was going to stay at a sinner's house they complained. BUT ZACCHAEUS STOOD HIS GROUND AND SAID TO THE LORD, "LOOK, SIR, I AM GOING TO GIVE HALF MY PROPERTY TO THE POOR, AND IF I HAVE CHEATED ANYBODY I WILL PAY HIM BACK FOUR TIMES THE AMOUNT" (10:8). Whew. If he squeezed a dollar out of you, he's going to give you four.

AND JESUS SAID TO HIM, "TODAY SALVATION HAS COME TO THIS HOUSE, BECAUSE THIS MAN TOO IS A SON OF ABRAHAM (19:9); FOR THE SON OF MAN HAS COME TO SEEK OUT AND SAVE WHAT WAS LOST" (19:10).

This is the beautiful thing about Jesus: When you looked at Him, you either turned to Him or against Him. The Lord never said a word to Zacchaeus except, "HURRY, BECAUSE I MUST STAY AT YOUR HOUSE TODAY." Did you notice that the Lord never convicted him or said, "I want you to make a public apology"? But Zacchaeus was so moved by the mere presence of Jesus that he made a public statement. And it was accepted by Jesus when He said, "SALVATION HAS COME TO THIS HOUSE." So seek Jesus out each day, even if you are up a tree.

Woman with the Hemorrhage

❖

Mark 5:25–34

There was a woman who had suffered from a hemorrhage for twelve years, which meant she couldn't go into the synagogue. She was considered unclean. You can imagine how weak she must have been. They didn't have vitamins and B-12 and iron pills and stuff like that. If you had a hemorrhage for twelve years, you'd be pretty peaked—not to mention the humiliation she suffered from her husband and her neighbors.

[A]FTER LONG AND PAINFUL TREATMENT UNDER VARIOUS DOCTORS, SHE HAD SPENT ALL SHE HAD WITHOUT BEING ANY THE BETTER FOR IT, IN FACT, SHE WAS GETTING WORSE (5:26). SHE HAD HEARD ABOUT JESUS, AND SHE CAME UP BEHIND HIM THROUGH THE CROWD AND TOUCHED HIS CLOAK (5:27). "IF I CAN TOUCH EVEN HIS CLOTHES," SHE HAD TOLD HERSELF[,] "I SHALL BE WELL AGAIN" (5:28). AND THE SOURCE OF THE BLEEDING DRIED UP INSTANTLY, AND SHE FELT IN HERSELF THAT SHE WAS CURED OF HER COMPLAINT (5:29). IMMEDIATELY AWARE THAT POWER HAD GONE OUT FROM HIM, JESUS TURNED ROUND IN THE CROWD AND SAID, "WHO TOUCHED MY CLOTHES?" (5:30).

Now when this woman with the hemorrhage knelt down and said to herself, "If I touch the hem of His garment, I shall be healed," that was a word. That word was a request. She didn't utter it out loud. Nobody knew who she was, or where she came from, or what she wanted. Suddenly Jesus turns around and He says, "WHO TOUCHED MY CLOTHES?" Her word reached THE Word, and immediately something happened—

immediately! I think that would happen to all of us if we had that confidence and knowledge and belief—belief—that the Word in itself is not like any other word in any other book.

Look at this again: JESUS TURNED ROUND IN THE CROWD AND SAID, "WHO TOUCHED MY CLOTHES?" (5:30). Now the apostles get a little bit edgy here: HIS DISCIPLES—probably Peter—SAID TO HIM, "YOU SEE HOW THE CROWD IS PRESSING ROUND YOU AND YET YOU SAY, 'WHO TOUCHED ME?'" (5:31). The apostles were irritable. To them it was a stupid question. With people pushing in on every side of Jesus, how could anyone know who touched Him? The Lord didn't pay any attention to them. HE CONTINUED TO LOOK ALL ROUND TO SEE WHO HAD DONE IT (5:32). THEN THE WOMAN CAME FORWARD, FRIGHTENED AND TREMBLING BECAUSE SHE KNEW WHAT HAD HAPPENED TO HER—see, the reason she came forward in fear was that she was unclean—AND SHE FELL AT HIS FEET AND TOLD HIM THE WHOLE TRUTH (5:33). And He said, "MY DAUGHTER, . . . YOUR FAITH HAS RESTORED YOU TO HEALTH; GO IN PEACE AND BE FREE FROM YOUR COMPLAINT" (5:34). Go in peace. What a sentence.

It's so hard for us to understand the power of the Lord. We do much more than touch the hem of His garment. We receive Him Body, Blood, Soul, and Divinity. So why is it then that we ourselves do not benefit as much as this woman did? There's power coming out of the Eucharist for us. There is the Word made Flesh. Sometimes you look at yourself and you say, "God, I've been in the same rut for how long?" But what we should be asking is "Has power gone out from Jesus? Has my prayer, my faith really released something?" You see, something is released each time you come into the Presence of Jesus. But most people don't believe it.

How little people change. All those people pressing in on Jesus didn't have the faith of that one woman. She alone in that crowd believed she would be healed if she but touched His garment. She was instantly healed.

Go through chapter 5 of Mark, the entire chapter, and read it slowly. Ask the questions: "Jesus, tell me, do You touch me? Do I touch You in return? Am I with You all day? Do I reach out to You in my problems, in my trials, in my aggravations? Do I touch You in my illnesses?" The woman knew. Jesus knew He had been touched. What a beautiful explanation of prayer, the prayer of one who has great faith. Power leaves Jesus by that fact. You don't have to argue with Him, or debate Him—you don't even have to explain. You just have to say, "Lord, I do believe you can do this," and there's a power that leaves Jesus.

He Wants to Love You

❖

John 10:16–18

JESUS says: "AND THERE ARE OTHER SHEEP I HAVE THAT ARE NOT OF THIS FOLD, AND THESE I HAVE TO LEAD AS WELL. THEY TOO WILL LISTEN TO MY VOICE, AND THERE WILL BE ONLY ONE FLOCK, AND ONE SHEPHERD (10:16). THE FATHER LOVES ME, BECAUSE I LAY DOWN MY LIFE IN ORDER TO TAKE IT UP AGAIN (10:17). NO ONE TAKES IT FROM ME; I LAY IT DOWN OF MY OWN FREE WILL, AND AS IT IS IN MY POWER TO LAY IT DOWN, SO IT IS IN MY POWER TO TAKE IT UP AGAIN; AND THIS IS THE COMMAND I HAVE BEEN GIVEN BY MY FATHER" (10:18). So the Father commanded Jesus to come down and save us, and Jesus responded.

It's important that we understand that there was a request made, and acquiescence to that request—meaning Our Dear Lord has free will. He says, "I LAY [MY LIFE] DOWN OF MY OWN

FREE WILL, AND AS IT IS IN MY POWER TO LAY IT DOWN, SO IT IS IN MY POWER TO TAKE IT UP AGAIN" (10:18). There's the mystery of the humanity of Jesus, and the mystery of grace in our hearts too, isn't there? We have so much grace in our hearts and yet we have free will—grace never interferes with our free will. Both the divinity and the humanity of God are present in this statement.

Jesus wanted to lay His life down for us, and the Father had commanded Him to do it. It's very important that we understand that when Jesus manifests His love, He does it on a level we understand: with free will. He *wanted* to do it. So if you have a problem with the love of Jesus, or understanding how much He loves you, just think of this sentence: He *wants* to love you. He has decided to love you.

The Canaanite Woman (A Meditation)

❖

Matthew 15:22–28

As the apostles and Jesus are walking along, a Canaanite woman shouts, "SIR, SON OF DAVID, TAKE PITY ON ME. MY DAUGHTER IS TORMENTED BY A DEVIL" (15:22). The apostles wait for the Master to turn around, but He continues on as if He didn't hear.

BUT HE ANSWERED HER NOT A WORD. AND HIS DISCIPLES WENT AND PLEADED WITH HIM. "GIVE HER WHAT SHE WANTS," THEY SAID[,] "BECAUSE SHE IS SHOUTING AFTER US" (15:23). HE SAID IN REPLY, "I WAS SENT ONLY TO THE LOST SHEEP OF THE

HOUSE OF ISRAEL" (15:24). BUT THE WOMAN HAD COME UP AND WAS KNEELING AT HIS FEET. "LORD," SHE SAID[,] "HELP ME" (15:25). HE REPLIED, "IT IS NOT FAIR TO TAKE THE CHILDREN'S FOOD AND THROW IT TO THE HOUSE-DOGS" (15:26).

I think to myself: What strange words. Is He not the Savior of all? Is she not coming to Him in deep faith? She is a Canaanite woman, a pagan who says, "TAKE PITY ON ME." He looks disturbed almost and says, "It is not right to give bread from the Master's table to dogs." I wonder what this woman will say?

SHE RETORTED, "AH YES, SIR; BUT EVEN HOUSE-DOGS CAN EAT THE SCRAPS THAT FALL FROM THEIR MASTER'S TABLE" (15:27). THEN JESUS ANSWERED HER, "WOMAN, YOU HAVE GREAT FAITH. LET YOUR WISH BE GRANTED." AND FROM THAT MOMENT HER DAUGHTER WAS WELL AGAIN (15:28).

I have never heard Jesus speak this way. He was so compassionate with Mary Magdalene, with Matthew, with Zacchaeus. This woman seems to be a good woman who is not asking for herself, but interceding for another. I go to the Master and ask, "Is there a lesson for me in this strange conduct of Yours, in this seeming lack of compassion?" He says, "Yes, I knew this woman's heart. Her deep faith and her compassion. But I wanted others to see it. I wanted her to be an example to all mankind of deep humility and perseverance. Even the rebuff she accepted in love. Even when she did not understand she kept asking and loving. Her faith increased each time I said no."

Isn't it the same way with us? I have asked Him for personal things, and for things on behalf of others, and have yet to receive an answer. As this woman was called by God to give an example of perseverance in time of trial, of deep faith when faith can be shaken, so God also permits trials and temptations and tragedies in my life to draw out from my soul those hidden qualities that are unknown, even to me. I know that He looks at me with a deep love, as He looked at this woman, when I persevere under trying circumstances, when I try to see the Father's love in everyone. These are opportunities for greater love, greater patience, greater humility, and a chance to show unselfish love for my neighbor.

As God treated this woman, He often treats me. It seems as if He doesn't care, but I know He does, and He only tries me as much as I can bear. As He told Saint Paul: "MY GRACE IS ENOUGH FOR YOU" (2 Cor 12:8–9). Whatever trial, whatever heartache you have, know that God watches with a deep love and He loves you from all eternity. In this trial, in this pain, in this suffering, when it has made you more like Him, He will tell you, "Go in peace. I have not seen such peace in all of Israel." Have hope.

The Death of Lazarus

❖

John 11:11–15

Jesus told the apostles, "OUR FRIEND LAZARUS IS RESTING, I AM GOING TO WAKE HIM" (11:11). THE DISCIPLES SAID TO HIM, "LORD, IF HE IS ABLE TO REST HE IS SURE TO GET BETTER" (11:12).

THE PHRASE JESUS USED REFERRED TO THE DEATH OF LAZA-RUS, BUT THEY THOUGHT THAT BY "REST" HE MEANT "SLEEP," SO (11:13) JESUS PUT IT PLAINLY, "LAZARUS IS DEAD (11:14); AND FOR YOUR SAKE I AM GLAD I WAS NOT THERE BECAUSE NOW YOU WILL BELIEVE" (11:15). Now you will believe. . . .

He knew that even among His apostles there was this element of doubt in their hearts and minds. I would suppose the same is true of even the holiest persons walking the earth today. Wherever they are, and whoever they are, they probably share the apostles' frustrations, their doubts, their lack of spirituality, and their inability to place the world and its cares on a spiritual plane. In a word, they are very "human." Like these rugged men, we don't always see the wisdom of God as He allows things in our lives. So often we question Him or we try to evade reality. Jesus comes out at this moment when the apostles are confused and ignoring reality and says, "No, this man is dead and I'm glad for your sake He died, so now you will believe." You can see here one of the hidden sufferings of Jesus.

One of the hidden sufferings of Our Lord was that nobody really understood Him. Very few people understand the visions, concepts, or lights of others; so understanding those of the Lord God is even more difficult. There is a hiddenness, an aloneness in Jesus that shows itself in this moment from Scripture. It's why it was so necessary that Jesus be united to the Father in His Humanity, because He would live a very lonely life. Outside of Our Lady, who wasn't always there with Him, He really didn't have anybody who understood Him.

We should make it our business to spend time with the Lord whenever we can; before His Presence and in His Word. We can never fully understand Him, but we can make the effort to grow closer to Him each day; to put ourselves in a position to be raised by Him and to see life as He sees it.

Will You Be Martha or Mary?

❖

John 11:19–22, 31–35, 39

AND MANY JEWS HAD COME TO MARTHA AND MARY TO SYM-
PATHISE WITH THEM OVER THEIR BROTHER (11:19). WHEN
MARTHA HEARD THAT JESUS HAD COME SHE WENT TO MEET HIM.
MARY REMAINED SITTING IN THE HOUSE (11:20).

I get the impression that Mary was kind of angry, a pouter.
She just sits there in the house as the Lord comes. This is
Mary, the great contemplative.

Now Martha, Mary's sister, is true to her character as she
appears in the Gospel of Luke. She was the one who said,
"Lord, why don't you tell my sister to help me. I've got so much
serving to do and here she is sitting at Your feet" (Lk 10:40).
Well here's that same woman, and she's got that same critical spirit. Instead of saying, "Lord I'm so happy you're here,"
or "My brother passed away," Martha says: "IF YOU HAD BEEN
HERE, MY BROTHER WOULD NOT HAVE DIED" (Jn 11:21). In other
words: "You've got some nerve coming here four days after he
died!" This is her temperament.

Still, there's a little glimmer of hope in Martha, and she
said, "[B]UT I KNOW THAT, EVEN NOW, WHATEVER YOU ASK OF
GOD, HE WILL GRANT YOU" (11:22). So she has faith in Jesus,
but she stops short before she can ask for something so impossible. Jesus says: "YOUR BROTHER . . . WILL RISE AGAIN" (11:23).

This is when Martha "the Enlightener" makes an appearance. Not only does she criticize the Lord; now she's going to
enlighten Him. It's amazing how often we try to teach God

something during our prayers—and that's what old Martha does here. MARTHA SAID, "I KNOW HE WILL RISE AGAIN AT THE RESURRECTION ON THE LAST DAY" (11:24). Which means: "What's that got to do with anything?" She never thought of the Lord raising her brother from the dead right then and there. She didn't say, "I believe that you can raise my brother from the dead." She says only, "I BELIEVE THAT YOU ARE THE CHRIST, THE SON OF GOD, THE ONE WHO WAS TO COME INTO THIS WORLD" (11:27).

Look a little further down. Mary, Martha's sister, comes running out now. WHEN THE JEWS WHO WERE IN THE HOUSE SYMPATHISING WITH MARY SAW HER GET UP SO QUICKLY AND GO OUT, THEY FOLLOWED HER, THINKING THAT SHE WAS GOING TO THE TOMB TO WEEP THERE (11:31).

MARY WENT TO JESUS, AND AS SOON AS SHE SAW HIM SHE THREW HERSELF AT HIS FEET, SAYING, "LORD, IF YOU HAD BEEN HERE, MY BROTHER WOULD NOT HAVE DIED" (11:32). You get the impression that she and Martha talked this whole thing over a few times during the four days that Lazarus was buried. They probably kept saying to each other, "You know, if the Master had been here, Lazarus wouldn't have died." They both say exactly the same thing to the Lord. Sometimes you can tell what people are chitchatting about because they begin to parrot one another in public. That's how you know there's been a little committee meeting.

AT THE SIGHT OF HER TEARS, AND THOSE OF THE JEWS WHO FOLLOWED HER, JESUS SAID IN GREAT DISTRESS, WITH A SIGH THAT CAME STRAIGHT FROM THE HEART (11:33), "WHERE HAVE YOU PUT HIM?" THEY SAID, "LORD, COME AND SEE" (11:34). JESUS WEPT (11:35). That's a magnificent account of the compassion of Jesus, and His emotions living in the present moment. Since He knew what He would do and what was going to happen, there is no reason for these tears, is there? He could have said, "Don't worry, I'm going to raise him up." But He didn't say that. He saw her distress and His heart went out to her: WITH A SIGH THAT CAME STRAIGHT FROM THE HEART (11:33).

And did you notice that Martha for some reason did not elicit this kind of reaction from Jesus even though she said the same thing? I wonder why? She's a little hustle bustle. She's always finding little flaws living on the level of the memory, while Mary lived on a level of the will. The Lord was moved to compassion by Mary's humility, by her faith.

JESUS SAID, "TAKE THE STONE AWAY." MARTHA SAID TO HIM, "LORD, BY NOW HE WILL SMELL; THIS IS THE FOURTH DAY" (11:30). Ah, here's good old Martha again. There she is teaching the Lord. You can plainly see her lack of faith, her lack of belief in a possible resurrection. She has no concept that Jesus is going to raise her brother. She's too busy enlightening the Lord: "Don't move that stone, it'll stink up the whole block." I wonder how many times we do that to the Lord. How many times have we talked the Lord out of what He wanted to do for us? How many times have we tried to bully God into doing our will instead of His? Throwing ourselves at His feet and humbly begging for His mercy is the lesson here.

In your prayer life let someone else play Martha—you play Mary.

The Raising of Lazarus

✣

John 11:44–53

THE DEAD MAN CAME OUT, HIS FEET AND HANDS BOUND WITH BANDS OF STUFF AND A CLOTH ROUND HIS FACE. JESUS SAID TO THEM, "UNBIND HIM, LET HIM GO FREE" (11:44).

MANY OF THE JEWS WHO HAD COME TO VISIT MARY AND HAD SEEN WHAT HE DID BELIEVED IN HIM (11:45), BUT SOME OF THEM WENT TO TELL THE PHARISEES WHAT JESUS HAD DONE (11:46). THEN THE CHIEF PRIESTS AND PHARISEES CALLED A MEETING. "HERE IS THIS MAN WORKING ALL THESE SIGNS[,]" THEY SAID[,] "AND WHAT ACTION ARE WE TAKING? (11:47). IF WE LET HIM GO ON IN THIS WAY EVERYBODY WILL BELIEVE IN HIM, AND THE ROMANS WILL COME AND DESTROY THE HOLY PLACE AND OUR NATION" (11:48). It's unbelievable. It's unbelievable what the enemy does, and that's why sometimes you don't know it's the enemy because it seems so reasonable. Satan makes the unbelievably unreasonable, reasonable. That's what's so bad. For anyone to see these incredible signs—a man walking out of a tomb—and say, "We've gotta stop Him," is just astounding. How many signs did they need to believe? How many signs do you need?

ONE OF THEM, CAIAPHAS, THE HIGH PRIEST THAT YEAR, SAID, "YOU DON'T SEEM TO HAVE GRASPED THE SITUATION AT ALL (11:49); YOU FAIL TO SEE THAT IT IS BETTER FOR ONE MAN TO DIE FOR THE PEOPLE, THAN FOR THE WHOLE NATION TO BE DESTROYED" (11:50). Here a very evil man is prophesying. It says here, HE DID NOT SPEAK IN HIS OWN PERSON, IT WAS AS HIGH

PRIEST THAT HE MADE THIS PROPHECY THAT JESUS WAS TO DIE
FOR THE NATION—(11:51) AND NOT FOR THE NATION ONLY, BUT
TO GATHER TOGETHER IN UNITY THE SCATTERED CHILDREN OF
GOD (11:52). FROM THAT DAY THEY WERE DETERMINED TO KILL
HIM (11:53).

This is why I imagine Jesus, knowing all things, sighed so
much on the way to perform this great miracle. If you knew
you were going to do something so great and that it would turn
people totally off—that it would be the cause of your demise—
it would certainly cause a heartrending sorrow. So I'm sure He
cried, not only for Martha and Mary—I'm thinking He also
cried because He knew this was the occasion the Father had
set aside, a last sign, the great sign that would force everybody
that was against Him to make their last ditch stand. They were
determined at this point to kill Him—at that very moment.

It is unfathomable that they would do such a thing after
witnessing an amazing sign like this: the raising of the dead!
It shows that pride can so harden your heart that you never,
never change. And that's what makes hell eternal. If you went
to hell at this very moment and asked the people described
in this verse what they thought now, it would be exactly the
same thought that they had then. That's why it's so important
that you give up your will in small things and accept whatever
God sends you in the present moment as an act of humility;
because if you don't, in time, you can get this hard, this stubborn. And finding God at that point is very difficult.

The Pharisees' Jealousy

❖

John 11:55–57

THE JEWISH PASSOVER DREW NEAR, AND MANY OF THE COUNTRY PEOPLE WHO HAD GONE UP TO JERUSALEM TO PURIFY THEMSELVES (11:55) LOOKED OUT FOR JESUS, SAYING TO ONE ANOTHER AS THEY STOOD ABOUT IN THE TEMPLE, "WHAT DO YOU THINK? WILL HE COME TO THE FESTIVAL OR NOT?" (11:56). THE CHIEF PRIESTS AND PHARISEES HAD BY NOW GIVEN THEIR ORDERS: ANYONE WHO KNEW WHERE HE WAS MUST INFORM THEM SO THAT THEY COULD ARREST HIM (11:57).

It's an amazing phenomenon how human passions can overwhelm the intellect, the soul, and the heart. When in the throes of passion, we are capable of almost operating by instinct instead of reason. If you look at these Pharisees, you'll notice something: they were living *entirely* on the level of memory, and in their imaginations. They imagine that this Man is in their way; they imagine that He would disrupt the whole nation and cause friction with Rome. They imagine that their positions as high priests are in great jeopardy. So they determine, on a purely emotional basis (there's no reason here), that the only way to solve the problem is to get rid of the Man. And so you find in this passage from John what happens to us when we allow ourselves to live on a memory level. When we live in memory there is absolutely no way that we can arrive at anything reasonable.

Why did they want to arrest Him? The motivation of these Pharisees was jealousy. Hearing that the people were beginning to like Him, they decided they would do away with Him? They were supposed to be the popular ones. When they walked down the streets, people would rush out and always stand so many paces behind them. They began to develop a tremendous amount of pride, and a tremendous amount of hypocrisy because in their human nature they had their faults and their failings. They had a lot of secret sins.

It was the Pharisees who when the adulterous woman came along were going to stone her because that was the Law. Now how did they know she was an adulteress? I'll bet when Our Lord started scrawling in the sand He wrote the days and dates that each one of them had slept with this woman. Who knows? But they did suddenly walk away, and that was not by accident. . . .

But by this time they had begun to concentrate on the popularity of Jesus to the point where they felt that Jesus was taking something that belonged to them legally. Jealousy is a *blinding* vice. It blinds the soul to any reason. It is *unreasonable* and once it begins to blind the soul, people become a threat to you. And the threat is: they are taking away something that's yours. Only what you think is yours is imaginary.

Jealousy is a fire, and it licks up the living water. Remember, the enemy, who is after your soul, plants seeds of jealousy in your memory, and in your imagination. You make them grow. He plants the seed, and then he stands back and laughs at you because you water it, you nourish it, you take care of it, and when it grows into a tree, it will choke you. It will choke you—and that's exactly what happened to these Pharisees. It began to choke them to the point where they couldn't see, they couldn't hear. They benefited absolutely zilcho from the graces and the miracles they were witness to. Every miracle made them want to do away with this Man more. And the last miracle was it! He raised Lazarus from the dead—and that really emptied their cup completely. They had to get rid of Him. There was no choice on their part at that point. This Man was too great and jealousy was consuming them.

The Anointing at Bethany

❖

John 12:1–8

Six days before the Passover, Jesus went to Bethany, where Lazarus was, whom he had raised from the dead (12:1). They gave a dinner for him there; Martha's waiting on table again. Martha waited on them and Lazarus was among those at table (12:2). Mary brought in a pound of very costly ointment, pure nard, and with it anointed the feet of Jesus, wiping them with her hair; the house was full of the scent of the ointment (12:3). A pound! Boy, she must have really laid that stuff on thick. I don't know how you would get a whole pound on anybody's feet, but I guess you could. I keep thinking about her hair. Isn't nard kind of oily? If it comes by the pound, it must be pretty thick too. Like a thick lotion. Her hair must have been greasy to say the least.

Then Judas Iscariot—one of his disciples, the man who was to betray him—said (12:4), "Why wasn't this ointment sold for three hundred denarii, and the money given to the poor?" (12:5). Isn't it strange that the question itself is a very logical one, and one that social people continue to ask today. "Why don't you sell everything and give it to the poor?" A man stopped me one day at the Network and said,

"Why don't you give all that money you're getting to the poor?" And I said, "Do you watch the Network?" He said, "Yes." I said, "Well, if I gave all the funds we get away, you wouldn't be able to see the Network, would you? You would be denied that beauty, that truth in your home, when you need it." He didn't understand; we are giving those funds to the poor: the poor in spirit. I think it was Mother Teresa who said that spiritual poverty was the worst kind of poverty—and in America and the Western world you see it everywhere.

So it says here that Judas SAID THIS, NOT BECAUSE HE CARED ABOUT THE POOR, BUT BECAUSE HE WAS A THIEF; HE WAS IN CHARGE OF THE COMMON FUND AND USED TO HELP HIMSELF TO THE CONTRIBUTIONS (12:6). SO JESUS SAID, "LEAVE HER ALONE; SHE HAD TO KEEP THIS SCENT FOR THE DAY OF MY BURIAL (12:7). YOU HAVE THE POOR WITH YOU ALWAYS, YOU WILL NOT ALWAYS HAVE ME" (12:8).

So you can clearly see God's preference. It doesn't mean we shouldn't do what we can for the poor; it only means that we must understand that the spiritual comes first, that devotion to Jesus comes first. Even our charity to the poor should spring from our desire to reach Jesus through them.

A NITTY-GRITTY GOSPEL

To me if the Gospel is not nitty-gritty and gutsy, forget it. You need to go out there and *live IT*. The Gospel is your marching orders.

The Triumphal Entry

❖

John 12:12–28

THE NEXT DAY THE CROWDS WHO HAD COME UP FOR THE FES-
TIVAL HEARD THAT JESUS WAS ON HIS WAY TO JERUSALEM
(12:12). THEY TOOK BRANCHES OF PALM AND WENT OUT TO MEET
HIM, SHOUTING, "HOSANNA! BLESSINGS ON THE KING OF ISRAEL,
WHO COMES IN THE NAME OF THE LORD" (12:13). JESUS FOUND
A YOUNG DONKEY AND MOUNTED IT (12:14). . . . AT THE TIME HIS
DISCIPLES DID NOT UNDERSTAND THIS, BUT LATER, AFTER JESUS
HAD BEEN GLORIFIED, THEY REMEMBERED THAT THIS HAD BEEN
WRITTEN ABOUT HIM (12:16). . . . ALL WHO HAD BEEN WITH HIM
WHEN HE CALLED LAZARUS OUT OF THE TOMB AND RAISED HIM
FROM THE DEAD WERE TELLING HOW THEY HAD WITNESSED IT
(12:17). It was because of Lazarus, you see, that they came
out to meet Him. That's important to know. This greeting was
very superficial. Very superficial. He had given the sign of rais-
ing Lazarus from the dead and they thought "Now this is the
prophet." And here you have this very sad sentence: THEN THE
PHARISEES SAID TO ONE ANOTHER, "YOU SEE, THERE IS NOTHING
YOU CAN DO; LOOK, THE WHOLE WORLD IS RUNNING AFTER HIM!"
(12:19). They had no desire to know He was Messiah, no desire
to accept Him as Messiah. He was not their kind of Messiah.
They wanted a political leader.

AMONG THOSE WHO WENT UP TO WORSHIP AT THE FESTIVAL
WERE SOME GREEKS (12:20). THESE APPROACHED PHILIP, WHO
CAME FROM BETHSAIDA IN GALILEE, AND PUT THIS REQUEST TO
HIM, "SIR, WE SHOULD LIKE TO SEE JESUS" (12:21). Now that's

a very beautiful sentence that you might use today: "Sir, we would like to see Jesus." Because we don't see Jesus, we manage to get all messed up in our lives. If we could see Jesus in the present moment, in our neighbor, in ourselves, in our actions, even in creation, our whole life would be different because to *see* Jesus is to be united to Jesus, especially in the Eucharist. If you really believe that the same Jesus in heaven is on that altar, then why don't you spend more time with Him when you have free time? It's not a kind of substitute presence; it's the same Presence.

PHILIP WENT TO TELL ANDREW, AND ANDREW AND PHILIP TOGETHER WENT TO TELL JESUS (12:22). That shows zeal. Whenever you're enthused about the Lord, enthused over His desires in your life, you always want to tell somebody. So instead of Philip going directly to Jesus, which he could have certainly done, he goes to Andrew. Some today say, "Go directly to Jesus. You don't have to go to any intercessor." Well, Philip went to Andrew, and I suppose it was for support. After all, if two go, it's better than one going.

JESUS REPLIED TO THEM: "NOW THE HOUR HAS COME FOR THE SON OF MAN TO BE GLORIFIED (12:23). I TELL YOU, MOST SOLEMNLY, UNLESS A WHEAT GRAIN FALLS ON THE GROUND AND DIES, IT REMAINS ONLY A SINGLE GRAIN" (12:24). It takes humility to be like that grain of wheat; to give your opinion, to prefer others to yourself. It takes humility to be guided, it takes humility not to be sensitive, it takes humility to put your pride in your pocket and die to yourself. It takes a lot of humility to have faith. A person who doesn't have humility lacks faith. They don't see God in the present moment. They don't see God anywhere for the simple reason that they're too full of themselves—they refuse to die to self. "I'm going to keep my little grain. I'm gonna keep a cover on it, and I don't want anybody to bother me." Don't worry. The Lord says it's just going to sit on the ground by itself.

Then the Lord doubles back. He knows how stupid we are and so He comes along and says, "ANYONE WHO LOVES HIS LIFE LOSES IT" (12:25). Now, if you didn't get the grain, kiddo, you ought to get this one.

What is it that you do when you're proud or you lack humility? You kind of nourish yourself: "Mmm, I'm wonderful, I'm always right, I'm always good, I'm always persecuted, I'm always this, I'm always that." It's me, myself, and I. You see, you're going to live with a trinity one way or another. The trinity is either me, myself, and I, or it's the Father, Son, and Holy Spirit. The choice is yours. But if you're not with God, you're with yourself.

So the Lord comes back again, hits 'em with the same thing, and says, "ANYONE WHO HATES HIS LIFE IN THIS WORLD WILL KEEP IT FOR THE ETERNAL LIFE" (12:25). Which means you count yourself to be of little concern. The world tells you exactly the opposite.

The world says, "I am getting better and better and I can do it." The world is a positive thinker. So you're never down on yourself, you never lose yourself, you're never one who dies to yourself. You enhance yourself, you make yourself great. What's the difference if you're not great, as long as you think you're great. So the world has totally contradicted the concept of the Gospel, which says, "Die to yourself. Die to this world."

Jesus then tells us: "IF A MAN SERVES ME, HE MUST FOLLOW ME" (12:26). What does Our Lord mean? How am I going to follow somebody who is infinite when I'm finite—Someone who is the strength of the world when I'm total weakness? How can I follow Somebody like that? It's His attitude, His life, His humility—that's what you are to follow. All you can follow is His example. We often say one thing and then we do something else. So the Lord said, 'if you serve me, you must follow me.' To serve is to preach the truth, to embody it, to be an example yourself.

"[W]HEREVER I AM, MY SERVANT WILL BE THERE TOO" (12:26). Wherever you go the Lord is with you. "IF ANYONE SERVES ME, MY FATHER WILL HONOUR HIM" (12:26). He then says, "NOW MY SOUL IS TROUBLED. WHAT SHALL I SAY: FATHER, SAVE ME FROM THIS HOUR?" (12:27).

Most people think when Our Lord had His agony in the garden, He was saying, "Let's forget this Passion stuff. There must be another way to save people." No, He says, "BUT IT WAS FOR THIS VERY REASON THAT I HAVE COME TO THIS HOUR" (12:27). There was no way He was going to change His mind in the garden. So what do you suppose He was agonizing over for three hours? Perhaps those who refuse Him, those who reject Him: the lost.

Our Lord is just talking to people. He's not demonstrating. He's not yelling. He just clearly says, "FATHER, GLORIFY YOUR NAME!" (12:28)—a very simple little prayer while He's talking. And boy, BOOM. A voice comes from heaven and says, "I HAVE GLORIFIED IT, AND I WILL GLORIFY IT AGAIN" (12:28). Which shows what? The Father is ever present. Omnipresent. The Psalmist says, "WHERE COULD I FLEE FROM YOUR PRESENCE? (7) IF I CLIMB THE HEAVENS, YOU ARE THERE, THERE TOO IF I LIE IN SHEOL" (8). (Ps 139:7,8). The Presence of God is everlasting.

The Last Testament of Jesus

❖

John 14:14–21; 17:4–20

If you want to read the last will and testament of Our Lord
flip to chapters 14 and 17 of Saint John's Gospel. If you were
dying, you would think hard about what you wanted to say and
would certainly remove any frills—leaving just the essential
points for your family to remember. This is also true of Our
Lord in the Gospel of Saint John.

He says here: "IF YOU ASK FOR ANYTHING IN MY NAME, I
WILL DO IT" (14:14). Of course, we know that if you do something in a person's name, like the ambassador of a country, you
fulfill the will of the country or the president regardless of your
personal opinion. You can't speak your mind, or you're not an
ambassador for very long. It is similar here.

Today we've denigrated this aspect of "asking in (His)
name" and we've become name-droppers. So now people say,
"In the name of Jesus," and then everything is supposed to
happen, like some magic formula. What the Lord is saying is
if you're going to speak in the name of Jesus, you've got to be
with Jesus; you've got to think like Him; you've got to be totally
united to the Father's will. You must be united to the Trinity in
your heart and your soul so that you're one with Jesus. Then
when you speak in His Name, you know what He wants. You
have a relationship with Him. That's why it's inevitable that
you will get what you ask when you do so IN HIS NAME, because you're united to the Lord and His will. You request only
what He wants for you. It's not a magic formula for prayer. So

when you speak the name of Jesus, be extremely careful that you are not just dropping His name but asking IN His will.

Jesus then says, "IF YOU LOVE ME YOU WILL KEEP MY COMMANDMENTS" (14:15). You've got to watch these little words in Scripture, these two-letter words. They'll knock you right out of the box. This "if" changes the picture: "IF YOU LOVE ME YOU WILL KEEP MY COMMANDMENTS" (14:15). So all of us have to wonder, "Do I love God?" Am I keeping His commandments? . . . The person who continues to commit adultery and goes to church, whether he's born-again or not, isn't loving God. You can't be a part of Satan's kingdom and God's kingdom at the same time. Light and darkness have nothing in common. So you can't do both.

Now the Lord says, "I SHALL ASK THE FATHER, AND HE WILL GIVE YOU ANOTHER ADVOCATE" (14:16). That means what? It means that Jesus is an advocate—and there is going to be "another" Advocate. So we have an advocate with the Father, and in Jesus and in the Holy Spirit—"THAT SPIRIT OF TRUTH WHOM THE WORLD CAN NEVER RECEIVE SINCE IT NEITHER SEES NOR KNOWS HIM; BUT YOU KNOW HIM, BECAUSE HE IS WITH YOU, HE IS IN YOU" (14:17). This is one of the most gorgeous sentences on this page. How do you know the Spirit? "BECAUSE HE IS WITH YOU, HE IS IN YOU." You feel the Spirit inside, you're aware of His working, you're aware of His inspirations, you're aware of His effect on other people.

To be aware of and attuned to Him is a gift from God. And that's why Our Lord says here: "I WILL NOT LEAVE YOU ORPHANS; I WILL COME BACK TO YOU" (14:18). Once He was gone, had He never sent the Advocate, we would be orphans. With His physical presence, He could only be one place at one time—only a few people could be around Him. But now, through the Spirit, He can be with everyone, at all times.

Then He goes on to say: "IN A SHORT TIME THE WORLD WILL NO LONGER SEE ME; BUT YOU WILL SEE ME, BECAUSE I LIVE AND YOU WILL LIVE" (14:19). So the world has seen the last of Jesus, but we can see Him in His risen life, we see Him in the Eucharist, we see Him in the sacraments, and we see Him in each other. We do all these things through the power of the Spirit. You could not see Jesus in the Eucharist without the Spirit.

"ON THAT DAY YOU WILL UNDERSTAND THAT I AM IN MY FATHER AND YOU IN ME AND I IN YOU" (14:20). Oh, the Trinity. It is the Spirit that makes you understand that the Father is in Jesus, Jesus is in the Father, They are in us and we are in Them. I suppose one of the greatest things we could do is let the Father love Jesus in us. Just allow the Father to love Jesus in us.

In John 14:20 we have the whole beautiful revelation of the Indwelling. There are so few people today who understand the Divine Indwelling, and they would never understand if it wasn't for the Scripture here. The cause of the Divine Indwelling is the Holy Spirit. He comes into our hearts. Now, we've got to know: How do you keep Him?

Jesus says, "ANYBODY WHO RECEIVES MY COMMANDMENTS AND KEEPS THEM WILL BE ONE WHO LOVES ME; AND ANYBODY WHO LOVES ME WILL BE LOVED BY MY FATHER, AND I SHALL LOVE HIM AND SHOW MYSELF TO HIM" (14:21).

So in order to keep the Divine Indwelling, you will have to be one who loves Jesus—and we know if you love Him, you will "keep [His] commandments." Are you keeping them? You've got to constantly ask yourself that question. In your quest for God, self-knowledge is extremely important, because unless you know who you really are and where you really are, improvement is impossible—contrition and true repentence are impossible. Spirituality faces reality. The world doesn't face reality—those living worldly lives can't face it. They have to pretend. So you have guys who tell you, "You're somebody. You can really do it." But the Christian says, "I'm nobody. Without God, I'm nothing," and rejoices in the fact that God is doing so much.

Look up ahead at chapter 17 of John. Jesus says, "I HAVE . . . FINISHED THE WORK THAT YOU GAVE ME TO DO (17:4). NOW, FATHER, IT IS TIME FOR YOU TO GLORIFY ME WITH THAT GLORY I HAD WITH YOU BEFORE EVER THE WORLD WAS (17:5). I HAVE MADE YOUR NAME KNOWN TO THE MEN YOU TOOK FROM THE WORLD TO GIVE ME. THEY WERE YOURS AND YOU GAVE THEM TO ME, AND THEY HAVE KEPT YOUR WORD" (17:6). He is referring to the twelve apostles here. "NOW AT LAST THEY KNOW THAT ALL YOU HAVE GIVEN ME COMES INDEED FROM YOU" (17:7).

There's a beautiful thing in here in verse 8 of chapter 17; it says "FOR I HAVE GIVEN THEM THE TEACHING YOU GAVE TO ME" (17:8). In other words, "the teaching You gave Me, I have given them." It's amazing Our Lord is constantly giving credit to the Father. Isn't it a shame how we constantly give credit to ourselves for everything? I did this, I did that. Psychologists tell us today you've got to have self-confidence. What you need is confidence in God. Whatever you have, you have from God. "[T]HEY HAVE TRULY ACCEPTED THIS, THAT I CAME FROM YOU, AND HAVE BELIEVED THAT IT WAS YOU WHO SENT ME (17:8). I PRAY FOR THEM; I AM NOT PRAYING FOR THE WORLD BUT FOR THOSE YOU HAVE GIVEN ME, BECAUSE THEY BELONG TO YOU (17:9): ALL I HAVE IS YOURS AND ALL YOU HAVE IS MINE, AND IN THEM I AM GLORIFIED" (17:10). He looks at His disciples and continues: "I AM NOT IN THE WORLD ANY LONGER, BUT THEY ARE IN THE WORLD, AND I AM COMING TO YOU. HOLY FATHER, KEEP THOSE YOU HAVE GIVEN ME TRUE TO YOUR NAME, SO THAT THEY MAY BE ONE LIKE US" (17:11).

It's very difficult to imagine the challenge the Lord gives us with that one sentence. You and I are to be one with each other as the three persons of the Trinity are one with each other. Then the Lord says, "AS YOU SENT ME INTO THE WORLD, I HAVE SENT THEM INTO THE WORLD (17:18), AND FOR THEIR SAKE I CONSECRATE MYSELF SO THAT THEY TOO MAY BE CONSECRATED IN TRUTH" (17:19). That means that Jesus is going to sacrifice Himself for them and they're going to in turn sacrifice themselves for Him. We also learn that Jesus is praying for us. We rarely think of the Lord praying for us. But He says, "I PRAY NOT ONLY FOR THESE, BUT FOR THOSE ALSO WHO THROUGH THEIR WORDS WILL BELIEVE IN ME" (17:20).

So you have an intercessor, a mediator in heaven, Jesus, continually petitioning the Father and atoning for all your sins.

The best definition of love was given to us by Saint John when he said, "God is love." That's why it's so important for us to live the life of the Trinity, because He bears fruit. This is what He keeps saying here: "I only gave them what You gave Me." So if you're living the life of the Trinity in your heart then you are able to love with detachment and trust.

The Arrest of Jesus
(A Meditation)

❖

John 18:1–11

AFTER HE HAD SAID ALL THIS JESUS LEFT WITH HIS DISCIPLES
AND CROSSED THE KEDRON VALLEY. THERE WAS A GARDEN
THERE, AND HE WENT INTO IT WITH HIS DISCIPLES (18:1). JUDAS
THE TRAITOR KNEW THE PLACE WELL, SINCE JESUS HAD OFTEN
MET HIS DISCIPLES THERE (18:2), AND HE BROUGHT THE COHORT
TO THIS PLACE TOGETHER WITH A DETACHMENT OF GUARDS SENT
BY THE CHIEF PRIESTS AND THE PHARISEES, ALL WITH LANTERNS
AND TORCHES AND WEAPONS (18:3).

Now you notice in Saint John's Gospel he does not give us
a rendition of the Agony in the Garden. Maybe he was humili-
ated at having fallen asleep.

Close your eyes and begin to see with your imagination.
You see Our Lord; He leaves the Last Supper and He walks
to the Garden of Olives. There's no account here of the three
apostles who followed Him. At a distance, you see lanterns
flickering, you begin to hear a little hum of distant voices; you
begin to hear these voices coming closer and closer. You see
the apostles finally beginning to wake up and wondering what
the din is about.

Now, you see Our Lord standing there looking in the distance, and then you realize that these are not His usual followers. These are soldiers, and they're a different kind of soldier;
they're the guards of the Pharisees. As you see these men com-

ing closer, you realize they have weapons, they have spears, and they're very determined and angry.

KNOWING EVERYTHING THAT WAS GOING TO HAPPEN TO HIM, JESUS THEN CAME FORWARD (18:4). There's a good place to stop. Our Lord knew what was going to happen. We would run. He went forward.

Ask yourself a question: Would I have gone forward or would I do what the apostles did and run? It was dark, He certainly could have run and He could have probably hid Himself. He used to hide Himself in the middle of a crowd when they wanted to nab Him or throw Him over the mountainside. You would have probably run like the apostles. But Jesus goes forward; He goes forward to meet them.

JESUS . . . SAID, "WHO ARE YOU LOOKING FOR?" (18:4). THEY ANSWERED, "JESUS THE NAZARENE." HE SAID, "I AM HE" (18:5). Now you see the absolute courage of Jesus. They don't even know who He is at this point, and Jesus asks, "Who are you looking for?" They should have said, "You. We're looking for You." But they didn't know what He looked like. Jesus said, "I am He." He enlightens His enemies. He tells them who He is. Isn't that a strange thing? He *enlightens* His enemies.

Of all the times to be thoughtful of others, you would think this moment would not be one of them. You would think that God would expect us to worry only about ourselves during moments of crisis. But look at the example of Jesus: all He can think of are His poor apostles, scared to death. And He says, "[L]ET THESE OTHERS GO" (18:8). Do you see the awesome compassion of Jesus? THIS WAS TO FULFIL THE WORDS HE HAD SPOKEN, "NOT ONE OF THOSE YOU GAVE ME HAVE I LOST" (18:9).

SIMON PETER—now this is a little touch of humor—WHO CARRIED A SWORD—and you wonder why he carried a sword

because he was a fisherman—DREW IT AND WOUNDED THE
HIGH PRIEST'S SERVANT, CUTTING OFF HIS RIGHT EAR (18:10).
The poor guy couldn't even hit the target, couldn't even reach a
head that was right there in front of him. He was not a soldier.
THE SERVANT'S NAME WAS MALCHUS (18:10), and JESUS SAID
TO PETER, "PUT YOUR SWORD BACK IN ITS SCABBARD; AM I NOT
TO DRINK THE CUP THAT THE FATHER HAS GIVEN ME?" (18:11).
Right now there are a lot of fervent Christians, true believers
who would like to get a sword and just lob off the heads of all
these liberals—just do them in. But this is a wonderful part of
Scripture that should calm their passions a bit. Peter reacted
the way most of us would.

Do you see the difference between Jesus and the apostles?
The apostles right away start running and lashing out at others
because things did not come up to their expectations—even
though Our Lord told them three or four times what was coming, they were caught by surprise. They didn't want to drink
that same cup. If you remember, the Lord asked John and
James and their mother, "Can you drink the cup that I am
going to drink?" They said, "Yeah, sure." He said, "Very well,
you shall drink My cup" (Mt 20:20–23; Mk 10:35–40). It is the
Father who gives us the cup, but we must have the serenity
and the love of Jesus. He knew all that He would endure. He
knew everything He had to go through. We have to go through
it as well, and we know it. This is not a time for swords or for
fleeing. It's a time to accept God's will and pray more, or when
the worst comes we'll do what the apostles did.

Judas and Peter

❖

Matthew 27:3–5; 26:75; Luke 22:62; John 21:7–17

The suffering of Jesus is complex. There is, of course, the physical pain. But imagine the spiritual and emotional pain. I would suppose it would be a very difficult cross to know the will of God and to watch people constantly oppose it.

When someone like Judas, for example, who was with Him for three years, saw His miracles, saw the fruit the Lord bore, and still could not recognize that He was the Messiah— that had to hurt. Judas became possessed by his greed. You see, the Lord was not chasing money. He was after the poor, He was after sinners, He was after the destitute. Judas may have come in with a good intention—I don't think the Lord would have chosen him otherwise—but when he saw the opportunities for gain, for *personal* gain, he bolted. It says in the Scripture, he used to take the money (Jn 12:6), that's stealing. So he began by stealing. Then he continued by satisfying that personal greed for money. When things weren't going as he imagined, he could have very easily said, "Well, this is not the Man I want to follow," and just left. That would have been sensible. Just go. But he decided to do away with Jesus. Not only was he possessed by greed; he was overwhelmed by jealousy and anger. The anger came from the Lord's inability to live up to Judas's image of the Messiah. Jesus was not fulfilling *his* needs. There had to be an anger in Judas beyond greed or disillusionment—an anger that ended with a decision: "I'm going to do away with this Man."

Look at this line from Scripture: WHEN HE FOUND THAT JESUS HAD BEEN CONDEMNED, JUDAS HIS BETRAYER WAS FILLED WITH REMORSE AND TOOK THE THIRTY SILVER PIECES BACK TO THE CHIEF PRIESTS AND ELDERS (Mt 27:3). "I HAVE SINNED"; HE SAID[,] "I HAVE BETRAYED INNOCENT BLOOD." "WHAT IS THAT TO US?" THEY REPLIED[.] "THAT IS YOUR CONCERN" (27:4). AND FLINGING DOWN THE SILVER PIECES IN THE SANCTUARY HE MADE OFF, AND WENT AND HANGED HIMSELF (27:5).

That's just awful. You have to understand why he committed suicide while Peter repented. Judas said, "I have betrayed an innocent man." But his greed and his anger prevented him from repentance. So what did he do? He rebelled against repentance. To the very end he rebelled against God.

Even his suicide was an act of rebellion. Some people say, "He felt sorry." No he didn't feel sorry. He regretted his actions because they weren't going to work. He didn't get what he wanted, so he rebelled against the Lord by taking his own life. He was the only educated apostle. He was from Judea, and the only intellectual among all the apostles—so he knew the Law. He says, "I have sinned." His reason leads him then to say: "I have done such a terrible thing. This is an innocent man. And I have betrayed Him." He must have seen Our Lord suffering in some manner. Still, he admits what he does, but instead of repenting for it, he only has regret—which leads him to suicide, the final act of rebellion against God. That's why he is condemned.

Peter, on the other hand, did not rebel. As soon as he realized what he had done, HE WENT OUTSIDE AND WEPT BITTERLY (Mt 26:75; Lk 22:62). He cried.

Remember that moment in the courtyard, when the Lord looked at Peter and the cock crowed (Lk 22:60–62). It must have been a look of deep sorrow and compassion. Peter couldn't take it. You see Peter's act of denial sprang from his weakness, whereas Judas's was an act of the will.

Look at what Peter does later. After the resurrection, John recognizes Jesus and says, "It is the Lord." But who gets to him first? Peter. The Scripture says he put a cloak on, jumped out of the boat, and went to Jesus. The Lord asks him at that point to feed His sheep and His lambs (Jn 21:7–17).

See Judas, who was full of regret and despair, left the Lord and hung himself. Peter who did about the same thing (not quite as bad, but bad for his office) ran to Jesus. Wherever he saw Jesus he ran to Him. Why? Because he knew that without Jesus he could not be whole. We need to run to Jesus in His resurrected body in the Eucharist. We need to run to Jesus. Think of Him daily. When things get a little hard, a little tough, a little disagreeable, when we fall, think of Him. Think of that agonized Body on the cross. Run to Him and repent.

Jesus on the Cross

❖

John 19:30

God's concept of love is vastly different from our own. Jesus on the cross is the Father's ideal—the essence of love. Imagine the depth of that sacrifice. See the Lord's bloody, mangled body and all the while He is being miraculously sustained by a loving Father until the very end. Think about it: There is no way that a human being could be intellectually alert enough to speak once a certain level of blood has been lost. The circulation to the brain would be nil. But you have to realize that it took the power of the Spirit to maintain Jesus until the very end, until He could say in a loud voice, "IT IS ACCOMPLISHED" (Jn 19:30). No mere human could have done it. And no one else in the history of this world could have redeemed us. So it was a miracle of the Spirit and the Father that kept Jesus alive to suffer to the very last drop of blood for your sins and mine. That is the ultimate in love.

On the cross, the bitter vinegar they gave Jesus was not meant to torment Him—at least they had some sympathy for the Lord. He tasted it, the Scripture says, but not until moments before His death. He wanted to suffer until the end. Now that doesn't mean that we should run around looking for pain. But it means we have to accept what God gives us in the present moment with love. Love through pain is a higher form of love. Anybody can love when everything is fine. What's hard about that? Love is proved by sacrifice.

Jesus demonstrates how we must love God and His will always. Loving God when things are sunny is loving what He gives you; you're loving His goodness to you. The real proof of love is when you feel dry, when you feel terrible, when things are falling apart around you and yet you remain loyal to the Lord and persevere in loving Him. Pain and sacrifice perfect love and transport it to another level far beyond mere feelings.

IN A NUTSHELL

His whole Gospel is daily living in, and total abandonment to God's will. It's very simple. Very simple.

The Thieves

❖

Luke 23:39–42; Mark 15:23

You know, I was reading the Scriptures the other day and it said that both the thieves crucified on either side of the Lord spoke ill of Him (Mt 27:44, Mk 15:32). Both of them. And one of them, after seeing Our Lord suffer so patiently and asking the Father to forgive His enemies, then says, "Jesus . . . remember me when you come into your kingdom" (Lk 23:42). He realized that only God could do that. I was surprised. You know you can read Scripture a thousand times and you always find something new.

Both of the thieves reprimanded the Lord and said, "You're supposed to be the big one, why aren't you taking us all down from these crosses?" (23:39). The other one said at some point, "Look we have what we deserve, but this is an innocent man, he hasn't done anything" (23:40–41). So somewhere along the line Our Lord's beautiful example of love and patience in the midst of great insults and trials touched that thief's heart. He found faith at the very end, and stole heaven.

The wine they gave Our Lord is another interesting detail in the Scripture. It was a bitter wine with a kind of narcotic in it to dull the pain; they gave it to a lot of the people who were crucified. Our Lord wouldn't drink it. He refused it, Saint Mark tells us (Mk 15:23). So there again, He deliberately chose to give His last drop of blood for us—which would have to take a miracle of the Holy Spirit because there's no way a man could endure such pain. You'd go unconscious. When the centurion pierced His heart, blood and water flowed out. When you reach the point that all the blood has been drained, water begins to come out of the body. That's why Saint John mentioned water. Blood and water came out (Jn 19:34). Every drop of His blood was shed, everything given for you.

THE LIGHT OF THE WORD

Nothing is greater than the mind of man, except God. Learn to fix the eye of faith on the divine word of the Holy Scriptures as on a light shining in a dark place until the day dawns and the day star arises in our hearts. For the ineffable source from which this lamp borrows its light is the Light that shines in the darkness, but the darkness does not comprehend it. To see it, our hearts must be purified by faith.

— SAINT AUGUSTINE

Belief in the Resurrection

❖

Luke 24:1–12

O N THE FIRST DAY OF THE WEEK, AT THE FIRST SIGN OF DAWN, THEY WENT TO THE TOMB WITH THE SPICES THEY HAD PRE-PARED (24:1). THEY FOUND THAT THE STONE HAD BEEN ROLLED AWAY FROM THE TOMB (24:2), BUT ON ENTERING DISCOVERED THAT THE BODY OF THE LORD JESUS WAS NOT THERE (24:3). AS THEY STOOD THERE NOT KNOWING WHAT TO THINK, TWO MEN IN

BRILLIANT CLOTHES SUDDENLY APPEARED AT THEIR SIDE (24:4). TERRIFIED, THE WOMEN LOWERED THEIR EYES (24:5).

Isn't it funny how we're always terrified by the supernatural? The people I meet on the street scare me more. Well, these women who went to Jesus's tomb were terrified. They're standing there looking at this empty tomb, when, all of a sudden TWO MEN IN BRILLIANT CLOTHES are there standing next to them (24:4). [T]HE WOMEN LOWERED THEIR EYES (24:5). I don't know whether the light was too great or they were just awestruck, but they lowered their eyes. Women in those days lowered their eyes, but today we'd probably say: "What do you want?" And reach for some sunglasses.

[T]HE TWO MEN SAID TO THEM, "WHY LOOK AMONG THE DEAD FOR SOMEONE WHO IS ALIVE?" (24:5). Now remember, these women are the ones who were there with Jesus throughout His Passion. They didn't cop out like the men did (except for John). These women were the faithful ones. So why do the angels challenge these faithful women? Well, *they're* the ones who saw Jesus before Pilate, they saw Him before Caiaphas, they saw Him dragged up the street, they saw Him fall, they saw Him crowned with thorns, hang on the cross for many hours, die, His body practically shredded just from the scourging—most men would have died then and there, but He kept Himself alive so that He could suffer more for you and me. They witnessed all of that and still they are looking among the dead for Christ, seeking Him the way the world would seek Him.

"WHY LOOK AMONG THE DEAD FOR SOMEONE WHO IS ALIVE?" "Why are you having these doubts?" they're asking the women. Then the angels say: "HE IS NOT HERE; HE HAS RISEN" (24:6). What a bomb that is. "REMEMBER WHAT HE TOLD YOU WHEN HE WAS STILL IN GALILEE" (24:6). So what does that mean? It means: "Why didn't you believe Him? Why didn't you stay here all night waiting for Him to resurrect? He told you three times. Why didn't you come earlier to watch and wait for Him? Why are you just asking where He is? He told you! If He told you, why don't you believe it? Why are you looking for the living among the dead?" When you look at this Scripture, you should ask yourself: "How much do I really believe?"

"REMEMBER WHAT HE TOLD YOU WHEN HE WAS STILL IN GALILEE?" (These angels know the whole story.) Remember "THAT THE SON OF MAN HAD TO BE HANDED OVER INTO THE POWER OF SINFUL MEN AND BE CRUCIFIED"—they explained the whole thing to the women—"AND RISE AGAIN ON THE THIRD DAY" (24:7). Don't you remember that? There's such a difference between our remembering the Truth and the actions that follow. Our knowledge and our actions—there is a vast difference between them. We know a lot, but we do little about it.

The angels are telling these women that there is no excuse. He told you! If you want to know what faith is, my friend, it's to believe in what He said *totally*. Nothing else holds water. You can think what you want, you can excuse yourself all you want, but when you face Him on that special day, you won't have any excuses. It all falls away like water off a duck's back. No more excuses. We know we should forgive, but we refuse; we know we should be loving and cheerful with one another, but we aren't; we know we are our brother's keeper, but we could care less. We know what the Lord said, but are we doing it? Well, someday you will answer *not* for what you knew, but for what you did!

And that's what the angels are saying here: "Didn't He tell you?" Haven't I told you 1,588 times to get rid of all the junk and rot and fussing and fuming in your heart and mind and soul? Haven't I asked you a thousand times? Haven't I asked you not to gripe, not to be critical, not to gossip, not to go behind somebody's back, not to criticize, not to judge rashly? Haven't I told you a thousand times? But you don't do it. That's what the angels are saying here. Didn't He tell you back in Galilee? What are you doing here, right now?

Well, THE WOMEN RETURNED—all excited, probably shouting, "He's risen! He's risen! He's not there!"—THEY TOLD ALL THIS TO THE ELEVEN AND TO ALL THE OTHERS (24:9). . . . BUT THIS STORY OF THEIRS SEEMED PURE NONSENSE, AND THEY DID NOT BELIEVE THEM (24:11). Isn't that something? THEY DID NOT BELIEVE THEM (24:11). They told them the whole story—the tomb is empty, He's alive, and they were reminded of the prophecies. Our Lord warned them (told them three times) "I will go to Jerusalem" and that's where Peter said, "Well, if you're going to be crucified, don't go." And still they didn't believe the women.

PETER, HOWEVER, WENT RUNNING TO THE TOMB (24:12). This is one of Peter's hidden virtues, because if you or I had denied Jesus so miserably, I wonder if we would have run to the tomb. Most people, because they're so self-centered and scrupulous and self-oriented and guilty, would not have gone, they would have hidden somewhere—"Tell me where He is and maybe I'll go see Him." But Peter ran. He was repentant and he trusted. HE BENT DOWN AND SAW THE BINDING CLOTHES BUT NOTHING ELSE (24:12). No Jesus. Still, Peter doesn't understand that the Master is truly risen. Jesus said He would rise, but they didn't believe it.

How often are we in the same situation? After the cross, after tragedy, after years have passed, I look back and see that that cross was good. I didn't see it at the moment, I didn't understand it at the time, but it was good. I can see how a particular decision would have been the wrong one. If God had granted this to me, it would have been a disaster. Why didn't I see it then? Why didn't I believe Him when He said no? Why didn't I trust Him? But we still have a chance. We can still look at Peter and the others and learn from their example, learn from their mistakes—that we must trust the Master now! We must believe what He says—that as He rose, we shall rise. God Himself will wipe away every tear from our eyes (Rv 21:4), and He will love us and we will know we are loved by God and by every beautiful soul in heaven. We will be needed, we will be cherished, we will be understood. We SHALL KNOW AS FULLY AS [WE ARE] KNOWN" (1 Cor 13:12), and we shall be happy forever because Our Lord is risen.

After he visits the tomb the Scripture tells us Peter WENT BACK HOME, AMAZED AT WHAT HAD HAPPENED (Lk 24:12).

But see, he didn't hear what the Lord told him. He didn't believe. Say what you want about the Pharisees, at least they heard what Jesus said. Remember, they paid three or four soldiers to stand outside the tomb. The Scripture tells us that the Pharisees instructed the soldiers, "Just say His disciples stole Him when you fell asleep. If you have any problems we'll take care of it" (Mt 28:12–14). Isn't it interesting how evil made arrangements to disguise the truth while those who should have known didn't believe at all? The Pharisees believed at least on some level—that's why they could make arrangements to disguise what was coming.

Let us believe as the apostles eventually did. Let us strive to follow the Truth and to believe even when we see nothing.

The Road to Emmaus

❖

Luke 24:13–35

THAT VERY SAME DAY, TWO OF THEM WERE ON THEIR WAY TO A
VILLAGE CALLED EMMAUS, SEVEN MILES FROM JERUSALEM
(24:13), AND THEY WERE TALKING TOGETHER ABOUT ALL THAT
HAD HAPPENED (24:14).

These disciples here, going to Emmaus, are a typical example of the wrong way to act. They had already been told
by Mary Magdalene and some of the other disciples—friends,
they called them—that the Lord had risen. And what did
they do? They walked away from the Lord! They walked away
from Jerusalem to go to Emmaus. What they hoped to find in
Emmaus I don't know. They just wanted to get away. They're
thinking: Let's leave this place. There's a bunch of nuts here, a
bunch of hysterical women. And literally, that's what they said.
And Our Lord was so kind . . . so gentle.

NOW AS THEY TALKED THIS OVER, JESUS HIMSELF CAME UP
AND WALKED BY THEIR SIDE (24:15); BUT SOMETHING PREVENTED
THEM FROM RECOGNIZING HIM (24:16). Their lack of faith is
what did it. You wonder how many times, in the very trials
we suffer, why we don't see Jesus? Because we're so blinded.
We're blinded by ourselves, blinded by the flesh, blinded by
the world, and sometimes blinded by the enemy—and that's
why we don't see. We don't see. And HE SAID TO THEM, "WHAT
MATTERS ARE YOU DISCUSSING AS YOU WALK ALONG?" THEY
STOPPED SHORT, THEIR FACES DOWNCAST (24:17). And Cleopas
says, "YOU MUST BE THE ONLY PERSON STAYING IN JERUSALEM

WHO DOES NOT KNOW THE THINGS THAT HAVE BEEN HAPPENING"
(24:18). He's very irritable. He's in no mood to answer a nice
question.

The Lord asked, "WHAT THINGS?" (24:19). Ha ha, Oh
Lord. And the disciple answered: "ALL ABOUT JESUS OF NAZA-
RETH . . . WHO PROVED HE WAS A GREAT PROPHET BY THE THINGS
HE SAID AND DID IN THE SIGHT OF GOD AND OF THE WHOLE
PEOPLE" (24:19).

See, that was their first mistake: They didn't believe He
was the Son of God. They heard what Peter said but they
thought, oh, Peter, he's always opening his mouth and getting
his foot in it. He always spoke and then thought. They believed
it was part of the same routine when he said, "You are the
Christ, the Son of the Living God." They thought, "Oh, there
he goes again." Many thought Jesus was only a prophet, even
His own disciples. They continue on: "WHO PROVED HE WAS A
GREAT PROPHET BY THE THINGS HE SAID AND DID IN THE SIGHT
OF GOD AND OF THE WHOLE PEOPLE; AND HOW OUR CHIEF
PRIESTS AND OUR LEADERS HANDED HIM OVER TO BE SENTENCED
TO DEATH, AND HAD HIM CRUCIFIED" (24:20). Here comes the
worst sentence of all (and their second mistake): "OUR OWN
HOPE HAD BEEN THAT HE WOULD BE THE ONE TO SET ISRAEL
FREE" (24:21). They didn't want a Savior; they wanted a deliverer. And I wonder sometimes if in our own interior life we
don't want a deliverer instead of a Savior. We want to be delivered from ourselves, from our weaknesses, from our faults,
from our imperfections—we want to be delivered from whatever is difficult for us. We don't want a Savior who makes us
know, in His infinite goodness, that we're rotten and fallen. We
don't want to know ourselves, so we don't look for a Savior; we
look for a deliverer.

Deliver me, Lord, from this temptation. Deliver me from

this fault. Deliver me from this imperfection—which may be the only source of humility you have, to know that you desperately depend upon God's grace to persevere in the least good thing.

Now, their third mistake: Not only did Jesus disappoint them, not only was He crucified by the leaders of the people (which means if He had been a true prophet this may not have had to happen), He was not going to deliver anyone. Now, to add to all these problems: "[S]OME WOMEN FROM OUR GROUP HAVE ASTOUNDED US: THEY WENT TO THE TOMB IN THE EARLY MORNING (24:22), AND WHEN THEY DID NOT FIND THE BODY, THEY CAME BACK TO TELL US THEY HAD SEEN A VISION OF AN-GELS" (24:23). These were men who had heard Jesus speak of angels. They saw miracle upon miracle: the two multiplications of loaves, all the healings.

So you have to wonder in your heart: How did these men get so blinded? But we're the same, we're the same—aren't we? We don't see our nose for the rest of us.

Then they said, "SOME OF OUR FRIENDS WENT TO THE TOMB AND FOUND EVERYTHING EXACTLY AS THE WOMEN HAD REPORTED, BUT OF HIM THEY SAW NOTHING" (24:24). What incredulity—but don't criticize. We do the same thing. We read spiritual books that say that dryness is the greatest purification there is. We read with great anticipation that we're going to go through a "Dark Night of the Soul," but man, you haven't even reached the letter D let alone the "Dark Night of the Soul." We're astounded that the Lord would dare to purify us.

You know what the Lord said? [H]E SAID TO THEM, "YOU FOOLISH MEN!" (24:25).

You have to realize He didn't say, "Oh, you foolish *man.*" There was nothing feminine about Our Lord. He was strong.

He said, "You foolish men!" He never said that to women, by the way. "SO SLOW TO BELIEVE THE FULL MESSAGE OF THE PROPHETS!" (24:25).

Are we also not slow, when we take ourselves so seriously? Whatever I'm thinking, it's gospel truth. If I'm feeling something, it has to be right. We're no different from these disciples going to Emmaus. No different at all. It's the same pride these men had.

The Lord said: "WAS IT NOT ORDAINED THAT THE CHRIST SHOULD SUFFER AND SO ENTER INTO HIS GLORY?" (24:26). Oh, now, isn't that kind of interesting? Is it not ordained that we shall suffer? Is it not ordained that as children of a Crucified Lord we shall be crucified in some manner, even if only upon a splinter? A splinter. It's going to be terrible if we meet the Lord and He says, "You couldn't carry my splinter. You couldn't carry my splinter." When pain appears in my life I must understand that if it was necessary in His life, it is more necessary in mine. There is so much within me that must be brought out, and in the crucible of suffering, everything is purified. THEN, STARTING WITH MOSES AND GOING THROUGH ALL THE PROPHETS, HE EXPLAINED TO THEM THE PASSAGES THROUGHOUT THE SCRIPTURES THAT WERE ABOUT HIMSELF (24:27).

WHEN THEY DREW NEAR TO THE VILLAGE TO WHICH THEY WERE GOING, HE MADE AS IF TO GO ON (24:28); that's the second time He did that. After the multiplication of the loaves He told the apostles to go on and He would dismiss the crowd. They were so irritable by that time that the Lord said, "Look, you go ahead. I'll take care of them." Instead, He went to the top of a hill and watched these men battle a storm. Finally, He comes walking on the water and they're scared to death. He made as if He was going past them because He wanted them to cry out,

"Lord, help us." And so it's the same here, the second time He made as if He was passing them, BUT THEY PRESSED HIM TO STAY WITH THEM (24:29).

They said, "Ah, don't go. You know, we didn't see the light. We enjoy what You say. Come on, stay with us."

He says, "No, I really have to go."

"Aw, come on. Please stay with us."

"No, I really have other things to do."

"Just break bread with us. Just have some supper."

"Well, okay," the Lord says. What a beautiful thing for God to do, to make you want to want Him. See, at the start of this little walk they could have cared less.

The personality of Jesus is so fascinating because as we stray, looking for our own answers to our own problems, trying to discern how to get out of this mess—if we would just press Jesus and say, "Lord, You know I can't do this without You, stay with me"—He will.

SO HE WENT IN TO STAY WITH THEM (24:29). NOW WHILE HE WAS WITH THEM AT TABLE, HE TOOK THE BREAD AND SAID THE BLESSING; THEN HE BROKE IT AND HANDED IT TO THEM (24:30). AND THEIR EYES WERE OPENED AND THEY RECOGNISED HIM; BUT HE HAD VANISHED FROM THEIR SIGHT (24:31).

All of a sudden, they saw Him. What is so fascinating about this is that they did not recognize His human person; they only recognized Him in the Eucharist. How pitiful that after two thousand years we're almost the opposite. We don't recognize Him in the Eucharist. "Oh," we say, "if He would just appear to me once, I would know for sure," or "I would recognize Jesus." Do you recognize Jesus in each other? These men didn't see Jesus. They didn't want Him at that point.

So their eyes were finally opened, they recognized Him and off He went. Why? It's faith He wanted. He didn't want them hanging on to Him because He appeared to them. He wanted faith, and their faith was enkindled when He broke the bread. They recognized Jesus and all of a sudden they saw He was Lord. I've got to recognize Him in you. THEN THEY SAID TO EACH OTHER, "DID NOT OUR HEARTS BURN WITHIN US AS HE TALKED TO US ON THE ROAD AND EXPLAINED THE SCRIPTURES TO US?" (24:32).

THEY SET OUT THAT INSTANT (24:33)—they forgot their dinner, they forgot they had already walked a long way—AND RETURNED TO JERUSALEM. THERE THEY FOUND THE ELEVEN AS-SEMBLED (24:33), who said to the two, "YES, IT IS TRUE. THE LORD . . . HAS APPEARED TO SIMON" (24:34).

What a wonderful thing. He appeared to the very man who betrayed Him. Poor Simon. We only say "poor Simon" because of our own weaknesses and imperfections. You know what's so amazing to me: with all our problems and trials, we don't look to Jesus. When the disciples of Emmaus recognized Jesus, all of their problems were gone. Isn't that funny? When Peter recognized Jesus, all of his problems were gone. Why is it that ours don't go? Why is it that we wallow in the same darn things over and over and over: the same imperfections, the same weaknesses, the same idiosyncrasies—why is it we don't see Jesus?

"THE LORD HAS RISEN AND HAS APPEARED TO SIMON" (24:34). THEN THEY TOLD THEIR STORY OF WHAT HAD HAPPENED ON THE ROAD AND HOW THEY HAD RECOGNISED HIM AT THE BREAKING OF BREAD (24:35)—in the Eucharist.

So here are two kinds of recognition. The recognition of Jesus in your neighbor: Jesus has appeared to Simon—He hadn't appeared to them yet as a group. He has appeared to Simon, appeared to the women, appeared to Mary Magdalene, appeared to these men going to Emmaus—but they didn't recognize Him in His resurrected body. I would think that was because they were so obstinate. Isn't it strange that Magdalene recognized Him pretty quickly? She thought the fellow moving around the tomb was the gardener. She said (and it really is ridiculous), "Tell me where you laid Him, and I'll get Him." She's going to pick up a man nearly six feet tall—deadweight— and take Him away. Now, if that isn't the extravagance of love. That's Mary Magdalene. The women ran, they got so scared. Mary Magdalene was beyond scared. He said, "Mary." And she said, "Rabboni! Master!" Wow. And these men were walking with Him and talking with Him—He's explaining the Scriptures for Pete's sake—and nothing! Closed minds. Then Jesus broke the bread and there He was. He had to disappear at that point because the Eucharist would not be the Eucharist if He hadn't.

Man had fallen through a tree, and by a tree man would be redeemed. Oh why didn't they see it? And why don't I see it? Why is it so hard for me to understand that there are times in my life when pain is necessary if I am going to enter into my glory? If I am going to be like my Lord I must be like the whole Christ, not only the glorified Christ. I too will have my passion, and the glory to come. We must keep our eyes on the Risen Lord and our hearts will burn within us no matter what happens—for our God is risen. He is truly risen!

Jesus Returns to the Apostles and Thomas (A Meditation)

❖

John 20:19–29

IN THE EVENING OF THAT SAME DAY, THE FIRST DAY OF THE WEEK, THE DOORS WERE CLOSED IN THE ROOM WHERE THE DISCIPLES WERE, FOR FEAR OF THE JEWS (20:19). Suddenly there is a silence in the room. Everyone feels a presence. They recognize it. It is the Lord, but they are afraid. Right in the midst of them is the Risen Lord. They look at Him and their hearts pound within them. They are so afraid they dare not say a word. And they are ashamed. The Lord looks at them and He says, "PEACE BE WITH YOU" (20:19). If I could only remember that one word when I am distraught as these apostles were distraught; when it is hard to have faith; when doubts assail me and hope seems so far away; when I am discouraged, if only I would look at the Master and hear Him say to me as He said to them, "Peace be with you."

Then the Lord SHOWED THEM HIS HANDS AND HIS SIDE (20:20). Each apostle and disciple looks at the glorified wounds. They're closed and yet you know that there was once a nail through those hands and those feet. Jesus kept His wounds to show us how much He loves us. He will always keep those wounds for they are the sign, a greater sign than the miracles He performed, a greater sign of how much He loves us. From those wounds rays of light and grace flow to you and to me. Will it not be the same with our pains? Will not the sufferings of this life glow? Will they not have their own beauty in heaven, and will not all men see what we have suffered for the Lord—what we have suffered with patience, with love, and with hope in deep faith? It will all be plain there.

THE DISCIPLES WERE FILLED WITH JOY WHEN THEY SAW THE LORD (20:20), AND HE SAID TO THEM AGAIN, "PEACE BE WITH YOU. AS THE FATHER SENT ME, SO AM I SENDING YOU" (20:21). AFTER SAYING THIS HE BREATHED ON THEM AND SAID: "RECEIVE THE HOLY SPIRIT (20:22). FOR THOSE WHOSE SINS YOU FORGIVE, THEY ARE FORGIVEN; FOR THOSE WHOSE SINS YOU RETAIN, THEY ARE RETAINED" (20:23).

THOMAS, CALLED THE TWIN, WHO WAS ONE OF THE TWELVE, WAS NOT WITH THEM WHEN JESUS CAME (20:24). WHEN THE DISCIPLES SAID, "WE HAVE SEEN THE LORD," HE ANSWERED, "UNLESS I SEE THE HOLES THAT THE NAILS MADE IN HIS HANDS AND CAN PUT MY FINGER INTO THE HOLES THEY MADE, AND UN- LESS I CAN PUT MY HAND INTO HIS SIDE, I REFUSE TO BELIEVE" (20:25).

Thomas is sure that these men are so distraught that they only imagine they saw Him. Their love for the Master was so great; they just think they saw Him. It couldn't be. That Man was so mangled. . . . He bled to death. He cannot, cannot, be alive. Thomas looks at the apostles and the disciples with disgust and he says, "UNLESS I SEE THE HOLES THAT THE NAILS MADE IN HIS HANDS AND CAN PUT MY FINGER INTO THE HOLES THEY MADE, AND UNLESS I CAN PUT MY HAND INTO HIS SIDE, I REFUSE TO BELIEVE." I look at Thomas and I think to myself, "I know. I have been incredulous so often, and I wish I hadn't been."

EIGHT DAYS LATER THE DISCIPLES WERE IN THE HOUSE AGAIN AND THOMAS WAS WITH THEM. THE DOORS WERE CLOSED, BUT JESUS CAME IN AND STOOD AMONG THEM. "PEACE BE WITH

YOU[,]" HE SAID (20:26). THEN HE SPOKE TO THOMAS, "PUT YOUR FINGER HERE; LOOK, HERE ARE MY HANDS. GIVE ME YOUR HAND; PUT IT INTO MY SIDE. DOUBT NO LONGER BUT BELIEVE" (20:27). Thomas falls to his knees. He will not feel those wounds. He knows indeed it is the Master.

THOMAS REPLIED, "MY LORD AND MY GOD!" (20:28). JESUS SAID TO HIM: "YOU BELIEVE BECAUSE YOU CAN SEE ME. HAPPY ARE THOSE WHO HAVE NOT SEEN AND YET BELIEVE" (20:29). I realize what a tremendous gift faith is. I have not seen Him, but I believe that He is risen, that He died for me, that He rose for me and that He lives within me.

CONTEMPLATION AND BEARING FRUIT

Contemplation is to be lost in the awesome wonder of God. I think that's one of the best definitions of contemplation. The whole reality, and necessity, of pondering the Word of God is so that Jesus might "live in me and I in Him." It implies that some live "in" Him and others do not. . . . He just didn't say, "Whoever remains *with* me, bears fruit in plenty." No. He says, "Whoever remains *in* me" (Jn 15:5). That's sanctifying grace, but I must remain *in* Him by the perfect accomplishment of His will.

If I do that, I have all the freedom and clarity of mind to ponder the truths of God. Otherwise your mind is cluttered with somebody or something else. Most of the time we run around with cluttered minds, and even when we come to prayer we complain that we can't pray. We're distracted.

(Sometimes we try so hard that we don't live in God; we

live in ourselves. We're so easily tempted to think of ourselves, or our comfort, that God becomes an afterthought. The worst thing during temptation is to think about it; because the more you think about it, the worse it gets.)

Prayer is important, because the fruit of prayer is love. The fruit that God bears in us is always the fruit of love. I can have all kinds of motivations for doing things or not doing things, but if the fruit is love, I can be sure that God bore it in me. Evil is also fruit; it's just bad fruit. Everything we do will bear fruit. The only way we can bear good fruit—because the Lord said, "without Me you do nothing"—is to remain in Jesus. Prayer, the sacraments, and contemplation of His Word are the only ways to remain *in* Him throughout the day.

THE MIRROR

When it comes time to live the Scripture you are looking at the *mirror of Jesus*. When you put yourself in front of that mirror, you know how you should be acting at every moment of your life.

Throwing Your Net Out

❖

John 21:4–7

Did you ever read chapter 21 of Saint John's Gospel? Do you realize that there is not one place in Scripture where the apostles caught fish without the Lord doing it for them? Look at this Scripture and you will know why God chose them and what He is looking for today.

Now, imagine you are one of the apostles: you've fished all night, you're soaking wet, and you've caught nothing. As you come to shore there is a stranger there, and He says, "HAVE YOU CAUGHT ANYTHING, FRIENDS?" (21:5). Can you imagine what you would say to that? My Italian temper would have gone right off the charts. I would have said, "I didn't go fishing," or "It's none of your business." I'm talking to a stranger after all; I don't know it's Jesus. Anything but the truth, never admit failure—that's the world today. But you know what Peter did? He said, "No, we didn't catch a thing." Very simple. He had something we don't have today. He had honesty and integrity.

The stranger says to them, "THROW THE NET OUT TO STARBOARD AND YOU'LL FIND SOMETHING" (21:6). This is totally unreasonable. God was asking them to do three ridiculous things: throw their net on the starboard side, in shallow water, at the wrong time of day. And they did it! They were simple men who were not afraid to do the ridiculous—they were dodos! What did they have to lose? They admitted their failure.

You see God is not looking for the successful and the competent who can do it on their own. He is looking for people like you and me.

If God were to say to you right now: "Throw your net on the starboard side of the boat," would you cling to it saying, "Oh Lord, the timing is not right"? Or would you say, "Lord, I just couldn't do that, people will think I'm nuts"? You have to be willing, in your interior life, to throw your net on the starboard side every day of your life. There's going to be a lot of shallow water and wrong timing. But you'll have the thrill of knowing that He does it all.

There were so many fish in the apostles' net that they could not pull them all in. At that point, John said, "IT IS THE LORD" (21:7). And here is a strange phenomenon: As soon as the net was full, as soon as they realized they had nothing to do with the catch except to be obedient—suddenly the fish were no longer important. It says that Peter (how I love Peter; I think he had to be an Italian Jew), Peter throws a cloak around himself, because he had practically nothing on, and leapt into the water to see Jesus. He didn't care how he looked. He didn't care what people would say. He wanted to get to Jesus and would use any means to get there.

Do you understand what God tries to do in your life sometimes? He is telling you to "Let go. Don't hang on. I'll take care of your future and your past. You let go." Throw your net and let Him fill it. Feel the thrill that must have been in the apostles' hearts on that magnificent day. They had an empty net and they kept doing the ridiculous and God kept filling it. It's only when we refuse to throw the net over that we catch nothing.

A Breakfast of Effort and Desire

❖

John 21:10–12

It says when they came to shore there was some bread there and a charcoal fire and fish cooking. JESUS SAID TO THEM, "COME AND HAVE BREAKFAST" (21:12). Isn't that tremendous? Jesus cooked breakfast for His apostles. Doesn't that tell you something? You see how human Jesus is, even after the resurrection? With His glorified body He's making breakfast. Isn't that fantastic? Tomorrow morning think about that and really savor your bacon and eggs. Jesus is totally unselfish. He looks at the apostles and says, "BRING SOME OF THE FISH YOU HAVE JUST CAUGHT" (21:10). Who caught what? He told them how, when, and where, then He put the fish in the net. But the apostles caught the fish. Jesus did it all, and the apostles did it all. They both had a part. In our lives it's very important for us to admit that all of the successes, all of the good in our lives, was put there by God. Sure you play a part, but so does He.

It seems to me that in our spiritual lives we don't have that deep reality of the invisible. Saint Paul says in Second Corinthians: "WE HAVE NO EYES FOR THINGS THAT ARE VISIBLE, BUT ONLY FOR THINGS THAT ARE INVISIBLE; FOR VISIBLE THINGS LAST ONLY FOR A TIME, AND THE INVISIBLE THINGS ARE ETERNAL" (2 Cor 4:18).

Now I want to go back again to that Sea of Tiberias scene after the resurrection. We know that those fishermen didn't catch one of the fish they ate for breakfast on their own. It was a miraculous catch. The Lord put the fish there. But the apostles had to do two things: They had to have a tremendous *desire* for a catch. They also had to exert *effort* to pull it in. So He could truly say to them, "Bring some of the fish you have caught."

It seems to me we lack something between the visible and the invisible in our lives. What is it that keeps us always in the same spot? What am I failing to do that keeps the Spirit from permeating my whole being? The Sea of Tiberias scene has the secret: We lack desire and we lack effort. We are either all effort and no desire or vice versa. We must right this imbalance and apply both effort and desire to do God's will.

The Ascension and the
Descent of the Holy Spirit

❖

Acts 1:3–14; 2:1–3

Lets look at the Acts of the Apostles. Tradition tells us that Acts was written by Saint Luke. This book really gives us a sense of what the early Church was truly like.

HE HAD SHOWN HIMSELF ALIVE TO THEM AFTER HIS PASSION BY MANY DEMONSTRATIONS: FOR FORTY DAYS HE HAD CONTINUED TO APPEAR TO THEM AND TELL THEM ABOUT THE KINGDOM OF GOD (1:3). You know we just can't imagine being with the Lord in His Risen Body, and having Him give us instructions in the faith. Of course, at Mass you're at Calvary, and at communion, you're at the resurrection. Throughout your day, He's teaching you all day long. We don't always like the lessons He teaches. We don't always like what He's saying, but, nonetheless, He does speak to us through the events and the situations and the people we encounter.

WHEN HE HAD BEEN AT TABLE WITH THEM, HE HAD TOLD THEM NOT TO LEAVE JERUSALEM, BUT TO WAIT THERE FOR WHAT THE FATHER HAD PROMISED. "IT IS[,]" HE HAD SAID[,] "WHAT YOU HAVE HEARD ME SPEAK ABOUT (1:4): JOHN BAPTISED WITH WATER BUT YOU . . . WILL BE BAPTISED WITH THE HOLY SPIRIT" (1:5).

After forty days with Our Lord, they ask Him an amazing question. They said, "LORD, HAS THE TIME COME? ARE YOU GOING TO RESTORE THE KINGDOM TO ISRAEL?" (1:6). Now, we know we should never be discouraged about our ignoramus condition after hearing these apostles speak. They are as unenlightened as we are—maybe worse. That is kind of an encouragement. The Lord said, "IT IS NOT FOR YOU TO KNOW TIMES OR DATES THAT THE FATHER HAS DECIDED BY HIS OWN AUTHORITY (1:7), BUT YOU WILL RECEIVE POWER WHEN THE HOLY SPIRIT COMES ON YOU, AND THEN YOU WILL BE MY WITNESSES . . . TO THE ENDS OF THE EARTH" (1:8).

Then along comes another shock to these poor men. You know, you just have to feel sorry for them. I don't know what they thought was going to happen, but they could never have thought THIS would happen. All of a sudden the Lord starts rising up. HE WAS LIFTED UP WHILE THEY LOOKED ON, AND A CLOUD TOOK HIM FROM THEIR SIGHT (1:9). What is this cloud? Spirit. The Spirit always comes in a cloud. The Holy Spirit is a favorite theme of Saint Luke.

SO FROM THE MOUNT OF OLIVES, AS IT IS CALLED, THEY WENT BACK TO JERUSALEM (1:12), . . . AND WHEN THEY REACHED THE CITY THEY WENT TO THE UPPER ROOM WHERE THEY WERE STAYING (1:13); AND THEY JOINED IN CONTINUOUS PRAYER, TOGETHER WITH SEVERAL WOMEN, INCLUDING MARY THE MOTHER OF JESUS, AND WITH HIS BROTHERS (1:14)—which means Jesus's cousins. Joseph had brothers and sisters; Mary must have had aunts, who had, in turn, cousins.

WHEN PENTECOST DAY CAME ROUND, THEY HAD ALL MET IN ONE ROOM (2:1), WHEN SUDDENLY THEY HEARD WHAT SOUNDED LIKE A POWERFUL WIND FROM HEAVEN, THE NOISE OF WHICH FILLED THE ENTIRE HOUSE IN WHICH THEY WERE SITTING (2:2). They weren't praying on their knees. They were probably sitting around chitchatting, wondering what was going to happen. Somebody probably said, "Well, we've been here nine days. How long are we gonna stay in this place?" One of the others may have said, "What's the difference? You got someplace to go?" This is the first novena. [A]ND SOMETHING APPEARED TO THEM THAT SEEMED LIKE TONGUES OF FIRE; THESE SEPARATED AND CAME TO REST ON THE HEAD OF EACH OF THEM (2:3).

When Jesus sent His Spirit, He really sent His love upon the apostles. The Holy Spirit is the love the Father has for the Son, and the love the Son has for the Father. That is what Jesus left: He left His love for us. And that Spirit, that love that loves in me, is fruitful when I begin to imitate it. If my actions are loving, my words are loving, my thoughts are loving—then the Spirit reigns in my life.

His body went up to heaven but the Spirit became a fire. That's what love is; love is a fire; it gives people the grace to be martyrs, the grace to do great things, the grace to be heroic in virtue. Love is a force.

Love was the most important thing in the lives of the saints. They judged everything in their lives by love. They didn't judge by justice or truth or weakness or strength—they asked one question: Was I loving? Everybody is a lover, if you get out of the way. Because you're made by Love to love—so don't ever say "I can't love." You may love differently than others, but God made you and created you to be a lover.

The Spirit, I believe, came as a fire because nothing survives in a fire. Nothing brash, nothing rough—nothing survives a fire. When this fire came upon the apostles, weak men were made strong, frightened people were made courageous, timid people were made bold, the fearful were made so brave. Remember, all of these people were hiding for nine days in a locked room. Just imagine yourselves now, all of us locked in two rooms for nine solid days. You'd be chewing each other up.

So why did the Lord come as a fire? What does a fire do? It did exactly what it was sent to do: it consumed all of the dross, all the dust, all the sins, all the weaknesses of these apostles, and turned them around—because love consumes, and that's what fire does. Fire like love knows no bounds. You can see this at Pentecost when you read the Acts of the Apostles. The fire that came upon their heads consumed their hard-heartedness, their weaknesses, their fear, and their lukewarmness. Pentecost is an influx of Someone Who is Love.

The Father is God, and the Son is God, and the Spirit is God. So there's only one God, and only one Spirit, and there's only one Love expressed in different ways—expressed by the Father, expressed by the Son, expressed by the Spirit—but it never ceases being one Love. So when we take our love and we allow the Spirit to burn up our frailties, we live in Love, and we live by Love, and we live through Love. The Spirit and I become one, because I disappear and He takes over—and that's what happened at Pentecost.

The Invisible Reality of the Holy Spirit

❖

Acts 2:13, 15

Here are men and women in the upper room, scared to death. The doors are bolted out of fear! In comes the Holy Spirit who permeates each one of them and leaves a visible sign of an invisible reality: a tongue of fire over each apostle.

They unbolt the door, go out, and they were so filled with God that they appeared to be drunk. Some of the people seeing them after this little experience said, "THEY HAVE BEEN DRINKING TOO MUCH NEW WINE" (2:13). You know how drunks look? They're silly, they can't walk straight, they might be dancing. The apostles were so filled with God and joy that they appeared drunk. They had to be doing something for the people in town to think they were loaded. The Spirit took such hold of them that they were completely changed into new people, like a new birth. They were born again in the Spirit.

Saint Peter then stands up with the eleven and announces in a loud voice: "THESE MEN ARE NOT DRUNK, AS YOU IMAGINE. . . . ON THE CONTRARY, THIS IS WHAT THE PROPHET SPOKE OF: IN THE DAYS TO COME — IT IS THE LORD WHO SPEAKS — I WILL POUR OUT MY SPIRIT ON ALL MANKIND" (2:15).

The Lord after His resurrection breathed upon the apostles and told them to receive the Holy Spirit. They had the Holy Spirit before Pentecost. What happened at Pentecost?

They received the seven gifts of the Holy Spirit. I think that on that day the invisible became visible. They had been with the Lord, but on this day the Holy Spirit touched their minds and reminded them of all the words and actions of Christ's life. They came out of that upper room infused with habits of virtue and the ability to constantly see the invisible. How conscious are you of the invisible?

An atom is invisible. Yet science tells us within an atom there are so many neutrons and electrons and protons, and so forth. Look at the power when you split an atom: a natural, invisible reality. The power can destroy a city. The Holy Spirit has a power as well—not a destructive power—but a supernatural, invisible power that is just as real as that of an atom. Call upon Him and ask Him to fill your life.

The Epistles

Mother Angelica's Notes on the
Epistles of Saint Paul
❖

S aint Paul is among Mother Angelica's favorite biblical figures,
and certainly one that she repeatedly turned to in her public
and private teachings. In the following excerpts she explains her
affection for Saint Paul and puts his writings in context.

God uses crosses—hatred, misunderstandings, pain, and
suffering—for the good of His saints. Saint Paul wrote all of
his epistles under great pressure. Every epistle was inspired
because a particular community was in trouble. At times they
were misinterpreting him, or criticizing him, or in error. Saint
Paul had to write to these people, and from the tone of the writing you can tell that the apostle was having a difficult time.

Everything that he had worked for seemed to be falling
apart. When he went to Galicia and converted them and moved
on, they began to fall apart. When he went to Corinth and converted them, and left, that community began to fall apart. New
doctrines sprang up and new controversies. Saint Paul was in
a constant state of confusion. So to read Saint Paul's epistles
and grow from them you must know that they were written
under pressure, often in a state of heartache. Saint Paul could
be very angry. He had a caustic sense of humor and a deep,
real-world faith.

The True Saint Paul, the True You

❖

2 Corinthians 5:11–17; 6:3–10; Assorted

I thought perhaps we would look at Paul in the Second Epistle to the Corinthians. Here we see a man who was not always appreciated by the Christians. He was not considered an
apostle by many. They thought him a usurper who had no right
to be called an apostle, and so he constantly had to defend his
right to preach God's word. I would like to explore with you
today Paul, the man: the egotist, the arrogant intellectual, the
humble Christian. He was a man who began his ministry in a
very odd way, by hating. God chose Paul WHILE . . . STILL IN
[HIS] MOTHER'S WOMB, he says in one of his epistles (Gal 1:15).
And in another place the Lord says, "THIS MAN IS MY CHOSEN
INSTRUMENT TO BRING MY NAME BEFORE PAGANS . . . AND BE-
FORE THE PEOPLE OF ISRAEL" (Acts 9:15).

But what kind of man did God choose in Paul? You know, I
think there's a secret here. I'm always looking for secrets. I think
all women love secrets; that's why we can't keep any. . . . But
when we look at this man all we can think about is "Saint Paul
the great orator." And he really wasn't that, you know.

During one of his great orations some poor fellow fell
asleep, slipped off a windowsill, and killed himself (Acts 20:9).
So Paul was the type of speaker who didn't always hold his
audience's attention. He was a little bit of a bore. One day
somebody complained to him and Paul got very angry. They
said he was "NO PREACHER AT ALL" (2 Cor 10:10). They called
him a half-pint (2 Cor 10:10). He was short, kind of stocky. Yet

this is the man whom God chose. He had great zeal for the honor and glory of God and a love of souls.

In his earlier life when he saw that some of the Jewish people were going over to the other side (converting to Christianity), his zeal consumed him. He runs over to the Sanhedrin at one point and gets papers authorizing him to arrest the followers of Jesus (Acts 9:1–2). He's going to do this right. If he's going to drag you away in chains, he's going to do it legally. And he does. We don't know how long he did this, but one day riding his horse on the way to Damascus, with only one thing in mind, "crush these Christians," a bolt of light comes along. God says, "SAUL, SAUL, WHY ARE YOU PERSECUTING ME" (Acts 9:4). It was such a powerful moment he fell off his horse, and he goes into Damascus blind. It takes Ananias to come and cure him of his blindness and baptize him.

Now we have this concept of Paul at that moment: rising up, getting back on his horse, going to Jerusalem, and beginning to preach. Well, he didn't. He went into the desert for three years to pray (Gal 1:17). It's about ten years before he begins a missionary journey to preach the word of God. Just imagine, it took time even after he was knocked off his horse; it took time for this egotistical intellectual to become a humble servant of the servants of God. In our lives we have the impression that after I have said, "Jesus is Lord," I've got it made. I just walk off and shine my halo every morning before breakfast—off I go being the most patient, kind, loving person this world has ever known. Boy, are we kidding ourselves? You know the world is full of potential saints. We're all potential saints. If we just understood that we're *potential* saints and will be until we die, we'd never say (as some do), "I've made it." Until you reach heaven you haven't made anything.

Now I want to explore a little bit from the Second Epistle

to the Corinthians and show you the man Paul, and try to show you how you are not only going to be saints, but how you're already on your way. No matter how miserable you are, or how miserable you feel, you're on the way.

There are some clues right here in the Scripture that show you how defensive Paul was, and I think they reveal the man. He says: AND SO IT IS WITH THE FEAR OF THE LORD IN MIND THAT WE TRY TO WIN PEOPLE OVER. GOD KNOWS US FOR WHAT WE REALLY ARE (5:11). You see, somebody probably didn't think Paul was too hot. THIS IS NOT ANOTHER ATTEMPT TO COMMEND OURSELVES TO YOU (5:12). Somebody must have also told him, "All you do, brother, is boast, boast, boast." They were tired of it. But he can't help it—this is the man. In fact, in one of his epistles he writes, I WOULD RATHER DIE THAN LET ANYONE TAKE AWAY SOMETHING THAT I CAN BOAST OF (1 Cor 9:15). Isn't that beautiful? WE ARE SIMPLY GIVING YOU REASONS TO BE PROUD OF US (2 Cor 5:12), . . . IF WE SEEMED OUT OF OUR SENSES—somebody must have called him a nut—IT WAS FOR GOD; BUT IF WE ARE BEING REASONABLE NOW, IT IS FOR YOUR SAKE (5:13). . . . BECAUSE THE LOVE OF CHRIST OVERWHELMS US (5:14).

FROM NOW ONWARDS; THEREFORE, WE DO NOT JUDGE ANYONE BY THE STANDARDS OF THE FLESH. EVEN IF WE DID ONCE KNOW CHRIST IN THE FLESH, THAT IS NOT HOW WE KNOW HIM NOW (5:16). AND FOR ANYONE WHO IS IN CHRIST, THERE IS A NEW CREATION (5:17). That's what you are, a new creation. Like Paul, you're a Christian, and God lives in your soul. You have a dignity above all dignities. There is no dignity in this world that can compare with the dignity of having God within you and being called to, and being in, Truth. As Saint John says, we are CHILDREN OF GOD (1 Jn 3:2). Just imagine that: children of God.

Paul goes on and tells them that WE ARE AMBASSADORS FOR

CHRIST (5:20). WE DO NOTHING THAT PEOPLE MIGHT OBJECT TO, SO AS NOT TO BRING DISCREDIT ON OUR FUNCTION (6:3). This is one of the obligations you have: to be a good witness to the faith; to do nothing in your life that might *discredit* the faith. If you yield to any passion habitually, you discredit the faith.

Then he says, WE PROVE WE ARE SERVANTS OF GOD BY GREAT FORTITUDE IN TIMES OF SUFFERING (6:4). Uh-huh. These are the little things in Scripture that we would very much like to skip over. Yet we're constantly griping about our problems, our tension, our pain, the disappointments in life, and all the people who are hard to get along with. And what are you to do? Buckle under? Look what Paul did. He said, FORTITUDE IN TIMES OF SUFFERING—you prove you are a servant of God by fortitude in suffering. You don't pretend it isn't there; you face it head-on and stand tall.

WE PROVE WE ARE SERVANTS OF GOD BY GREAT FORTI-TUDE . . . IN TIMES OF HARDSHIP AND DISTRESS (6:4); WHEN WE ARE FLOGGED, OR SENT TO PRISON, OR MOBBED (6:5). Can you imagine being mobbed? Being flogged, being hated? Just walking down the street and having somebody spit on you? If anybody did that to us that would probably be the end of our faith, our life, our hope, our love—we would flatten out in the gutter. But Paul went through all of it because THE LOVE OF CHRIST OVERWHELMS US (2 Cor 5:14).

Look at what Paul says: WE PROVE WE ARE GOD'S SER-VANTS BY OUR PURITY, KNOWLEDGE, PATIENCE AND KINDNESS; BY A SPIRIT OF HOLINESS, BY A LOVE FREE FROM AFFECTATION (6:6). You know we have a tremendous amount of affectation in our lives. I asked a woman one time, "How's so-and-so?" And she said, "Oh, I don't know, I never ask her. I'm afraid she'll tell me." That's affectation. Some people come up to you and they say, "Oh you look just beautiful." It nauseates you. Because you just got through looking in the mirror and you looked horrible. You've got bags under your eyes and you're tired. But they have this affected way of talking and you know it isn't from the heart. So Paul says we must practice A LOVE FREE FROM AFFECTATION (6:6), a love that comes from down deep and accepts a person as he is.

Do you really want to love God or do you want people to *think* you love God? Paul said we are OBSCURE YET FAMOUS; SAID TO BE DYING AND HERE ARE WE ALIVE; RUMOURED TO BE EXECUTED BEFORE WE ARE SENTENCED (6:9); THOUGHT MOST MISERABLE AND YET WE ARE ALWAYS REJOICING; TAKEN FOR PAUPERS THOUGH WE MAKE OTHERS RICH, FOR PEOPLE HAVING NOTHING THOUGH WE HAVE EVERYTHING (6:10). Now how do I get to that state, huh? It's beautiful to read. Beautiful. But now we come to the nitty-gritty living.

You have husbands and wives that bug you—well, you bug them too, so let's make it even steven. Don't forget, you are not only the bugged, you are also the bugger! Somewhere, somehow, somebody is under the impression that you are NOT God's gift to humanity either. This is life. I had a woman tell me the other day she's very unhappy because her husband's a salesman and he's constantly coming home with glowing tales about the cuisine he eats in all these restaurants while she's eating hot dogs at home. I said, "I wouldn't worry about that. Does he tell you the times he goes into an office and he's rebuffed by the executive who doesn't want his line of stuff or thinks it's inferior to what he's already using? Does he tell you about the nights he doesn't sleep wondering where he's going to go next?" Oh let's be real. Instead of thinking about how much you're suffering and how much so-and-so is bugging you, why don't you start to think: This is life. How am I going to become a saint with all of this? Because these things are never going to leave you, and you will battle your faults until you die. You can go to Timbuktu or Bangladesh and you'd still be there with yourself. You are your biggest problem.

In the Scripture you'll find hope to transform your life. Don't despair and don't think holiness is not for you or that God doesn't love you. Though you fall a million times a day, our Father will reach down and lift you up and teach you humility. . . . That's what holiness is. It's about falling and rising with God. If you reject God, it is you who reject Him. He never rejects you. God's hand is the last one to let go. That's the message of Paul and that's the message of Christ.

You see, I find the apostles' faults very encouraging. I like to go through Scripture looking for all the human things that nobody ever mentions—the disgusting disease that Saint Paul mentions in Second Corinthians (12:7). We don't like to think that Paul had a disgusting disease. He is supposed to be this towering figure, this great holy man, like that statue in Rome. Well, he might have had epilepsy. Can you imagine Saint Paul an epileptic? He might have had dysentery. "Oh, no saint would have dysentery!" some will say. The saints had dysentery and they had a lot of other things. This is life! They lived it with God, and so must we.

The Marks of a Christian

❖

Titus 1:5–15

Today we're going to look at the letter of Saint Paul to Titus, because it is seldom read. There must be something in Titus that keeps everyone away. It says, THE REASON I LEFT YOU BEHIND IN CRETE WAS FOR YOU TO GET EVERYTHING ORGANISED . . . AND APPOINT ELDERS IN EVERY TOWN, IN THE WAY THAT I TOLD YOU (1:5): THAT IS, EACH OF THEM MUST BE A MAN OF IRREPROACHABLE CHARACTER; HE MUST NOT HAVE BEEN MARRIED MORE THAN ONCE, AND HIS CHILDREN MUST BE BELIEVERS AND NOT UNCONTROLLABLE OR LIABLE TO BE CHARGED WITH DISORDERLY CONDUCT (1:6). Paul was very strict with the ministers. Not only did the ministers have to be holy, but their families had to be holy as well. SINCE, AS PRESIDENT, HE WILL BE GOD'S REPRESENTATIVE, HE MUST BE IRREPROACHABLE: NEVER AN ARROGANT OR HOT-TEMPERED MAN (1:7). This applies to all Christians because we all share the priesthood, though we don't all perform the function in the same manner. So he is telling us never to be hot-tempered, NOR A HEAVY DRINKER OR VIOLENT, NOR OUT TO MAKE MONEY (1:7). Today this is accepted and no longer considered wrong.

Paul says that the ideal candidate must be A MAN WHO IS HOSPITABLE (1:8). It is something that is indicative of a Christian. Now, sometimes we get the wrong idea of hospitality. We think this means that grandma, Uncle George, and your mother-in-law are going to come for Christmas and you have to kind of brace yourself for this awful trial. It makes for

one miserable holiday. Hospitality is not only inviting someone into your home, but it is inviting someone into your heart.
The essence of hospitality is to make someone feel that they
are important to you. It means showing a willingness to help
others no matter the cost. A Christian must be HOSPITABLE
AND A FRIEND OF ALL THAT IS GOOD; SENSIBLE, MORAL, DEVOUT
AND SELF-CONTROLLED (1:8). Most people have no sense of
these anymore. Self-control means that you have mental and
physical discipline. If more people practiced self-control there
would be true peace and less evil.

He goes on to say HE MUST HAVE A FIRM GRASP OF THE
UNCHANGING MESSAGE OF THE TRADITION (1:9). Don't forget, he
said "tradition" because when Paul was writing to Titus there
were no epistles. None of the people reading these letters had
any concept that we would later consider them Scripture. At
the time they were considered by some to be the letters of a
madman, a former persecutor of the Church. Everything that
Jesus did was passed on to them by word of mouth, gesture,
and practice.

He goes on to say there are A GREAT MANY PEOPLE WHO
NEED TO BE DISCIPLINED, WHO TALK NONSENSE AND TRY TO MAKE
OTHERS BELIEVE IT (1:10). What do you do with these people?
How far do you go with someone who is in error? You never
stop loving him, but at what point do you no longer condone
what he does or thinks? Saint Paul is quite clear: THEY HAVE
GOT TO BE SILENCED: MEN OF THIS KIND RUIN WHOLE FAMILIES,
BY TEACHING THINGS THAT THEY OUGHT NOT TO (1:11). . . . YOU
WILL HAVE TO BE SEVERE IN CORRECTING THEM, AND MAKE THEM
SOUND IN THE FAITH (1:13). So we must not let corrupt teach-
ers slide, but be clear and bold in correcting their errors. But
at the same time we must be charitable enough so that they
continue to listen and return to a sound faith.

Paul says, TO ALL WHO ARE PURE THEMSELVES, EVERYTHING IS PURE; BUT TO THOSE WHO HAVE BEEN CORRUPTED AND LACK FAITH, NOTHING CAN BE PURE—THE CORRUPTION IS BOTH IN THEIR MINDS AND IN THEIR CONSCIENCES (1:15). THEY CLAIM TO HAVE KNOWLEDGE OF GOD BUT THE THINGS THEY DO ARE NOTHING BUT A DENIAL OF HIM; THEY ARE OUTRAGEOUSLY RE-BELLIOUS AND QUITE INCAPABLE OF DOING GOOD (1:16). It's an awful indictment.

There are people, even in the world today, who are deliberately trying to confuse you, to ruin the Christianity that you have learned your whole life through. When they aggravate you to the point where you're ready to pop them they say, "Hey, a Christian wouldn't do that." Don't strike them, reach out and give them the truth. We must be kind to all, but know that there are some whom you must stay away from, who will never listen to you. Leave them to the Lord and walk away.

Picking Up the Pieces

❖

Acts 20:9–12

I love Saint Paul, but I'm going to deck him when I get to the Kingdom. Because I have often used him as an example of how human and faulty you can be while still achieving holiness. This little man was a terrible preacher and he knew it.

One day he talked all night and this kid up in a windowsill fell asleep—flopped right out the window to his death. Paul didn't strike his breast and say, "Oh I spoke too long." He ran out to this poor body splattered all over the ground and he said,

"Son, get up." Then he went back upstairs, continued eating, and preached the rest of the night.

He was human and he let God's grace build on that human nature. He knew what it meant to be holy: being faithful to the state of life where God has placed you, accepting everything as coming from the Lord, living in the present moment, and being enthused. We lack this in the Church today. Loving God is not a joyless thing, and it shouldn't be a passionless thing either.

Reaching the Promised Land

❖

Hebrews 4:1–3, 6–7

In chapter 4 of Hebrews it speaks of the forty years that the Israelites wandered through the desert. They were unfaithful to God. Yet it is amazing to me how faithful God is to us. No matter how unfaithful people are, God constantly pursues them as a shepherd pursues a lost sheep. He is always faithful.

Saint Paul says: BE CAREFUL, THEN: THE PROMISE OF REACHING THE PLACE OF REST HE HAD FOR THEM STILL HOLDS GOOD, AND NONE OF YOU MUST THINK THAT HE HAS COME TOO LATE FOR IT (4:1). The "place of rest" Paul speaks of is the Messiah, the new covenant, the new kingdom. They had gone through the desert to arrive at the Promised Land—the promised Messiah. Paul also says, WE RECEIVED THE GOOD NEWS EXACTLY AS THEY DID; BUT HEARING THE MESSAGE DID THEM NO GOOD BECAUSE THEY DID NOT SHARE THE FAITH OF THOSE WHO LISTENED

(4:2). This is one of the greatest phenomena I would say. You can go to any church and you will find that people week after week are being told the same thing. They are all listening, but they do not all *hear*. They never reach the Promised Land.

Every sermon you hear, everything you read should help you arrive at that Promised Land. Your heaven, or hell, or purgatory begins here. You don't just die and go to heaven. I see people in hell here; they do the same evil thing over and over and over. They are miserable. They spend forty years in the desert of misery, suffering, and spiritual hunger. They never arrive at that place of rest, that tranquility of spirit. Human passions and human greed keep them away. Saint Paul says we indulge ourselves. We think of our pleasure and our pet hatreds—everybody has one. And these things bar us from freedom of the soul. WE, HOWEVER, WHO HAVE FAITH, SHALL REACH A PLACE OF REST (4:3), Paul says. Is he only talking about the final rest? No, your eternity begins here. You are right now in heaven or hell. Most people hop back and forth.

IT IS ESTABLISHED, THEN, THAT THERE WOULD BE SOME PEOPLE WHO REACH IT, AND SINCE THOSE WHO FIRST HEARD THE GOOD NEWS FAILED TO REACH IT THROUGH THEIR DISOBEDIENCE (4:6), GOD FIXED ANOTHER DAY (4:7). Now, some would look upon this as predestination and claim that God looked upon everything and said, "You people on the left go to hell. You people on the right go to heaven." No. It's only that God, to whom all things are present, knows what I will do. Do you think it was a surprise that He chose Judas? Because God follows the pattern that He has set before all men. You as an individual must choose. And to choose well, Saint Paul offers this nugget of advice: "If only you would listen to Him today; do not harden your hearts" (Heb 3:15). Listen to what the Lord is telling you in each moment, watch what He is sending you in each moment. He wants you to follow Him, but He won't force you—and He won't impose a final destination on you. You do.

When you hear people say that there is no hell because God is loving, and being a loving God He would never condemn anyone to hell, that's a truth, but only half a truth. God does not put anyone in hell, God does not want anyone in hell, but they themselves will it. God loving lets you go where you want to go. The individual puts himself in hell. You see God didn't do His people some great injustice by allowing them to wander through the desert for forty years. If God gave you everything you wanted, He would not be treating you like a father. A father chastises. When God says no to you, it is a blessing, because He is acting toward you as a Father who knows best. When He lets you go, when His infinite justice allows you to go your own way, then you are in trouble. So long as God gives you some things and denies you others, rest secure.

We shall all travel toward heaven, but we shall not all arrive. Some of our pagan brothers will get there and we will not. Each shall be judged by the light we have been given. Remember, we are intended to arrive, so let's not linger in the desert. Don't hug your little passions: the bottles, the sex, the meanness, the greed. Stop hugging misery as if it were livable, leave the desert once and for all, and journey on toward the Promised Land.

Patient Perseverance

❖

Romans 5:3-4

Saint Paul says here, THESE SUFFERINGS BRING PATIENCE, AS WE KNOW (5:3), AND PATIENCE BRINGS PERSEVERANCE, AND PERSEVERANCE BRINGS HOPE (5:4). One would imagine that suffering could be of no use to our poor human nature. We don't want to suffer. We don't. We like to persevere, but we don't understand that suffering makes us persevere.

Perseverance in itself is a virtue, a moving virtue—it pushes you to keep going in the face of all obstacles. It's a very active virtue, and that's why when I read this I never cease to wonder how sufferings bring patience. We think sufferings make us impatient, but Paul says that "sufferings bring patience." During suffering we must accept what God has sent us. In that acceptance we find patience. And if we can be patient long enough, we are persevering. The constant giving of oneself to God's will, persevering through pain and suffering, is itself an act of hope, isn't it? Patient perseverance—what a beautiful definition of hope. No matter your condition, be hopeful each day, each moment, and remember that God perseveres in His love for you.

The Light

❖

2 Corinthians 4:6

In Second Corinthians Saint Paul says Jesus is the "LIGHT SHINING OUT OF DARKNESS," WHO HAS SHONE IN OUR MINDS TO RADIATE THE LIGHT OF THE KNOWLEDGE OF GOD'S GLORY, THE GLORY ON THE FACE OF CHRIST (4:6). We learn a few things here.

We learn, first, that there must be light shining out of darkness. This part is amazing to me: WHO HAS SHONE IN OUR MINDS (4:6). That's where the light is. We're always looking for somebody radiating light by their holy life, by what they accomplish, by what they do, by their virtue—aren't we? And all of that is fine. But what Saint Paul is saying here is when we talk about Jesus, it is THE LIGHT OF THE KNOWLEDGE OF GOD'S GLORY (4:6) that gives us light. So we take light from light.

God's Choice

❖

Galatians 1:15

Let's go to Galatians: GOD, WHO HAD SPECIALLY CHOSEN ME WHILE I WAS STILL IN MY MOTHER'S WOMB, CALLED ME THROUGH HIS GRACE AND CHOSE (1:15) TO REVEAL HIS SON IN ME (1:16).

You have to grasp the reality that through God you were

present from all eternity. He had you in His mind from the beginning. If you want to ponder something sometime, that would be a wonderful thing to ponder because it is beyond our realization.

It says here WHILE I WAS STILL IN MY MOTHER'S WOMB (1:15), He called me and chose me. Paul was specially chosen, as you and I are chosen. We cannot even comprehend "before time began." But to be specially chosen *then,* I had to be in the mind of God *before* time began. God doesn't do anything haphazardly. He's not impetuous. He doesn't say, "Oh I think I'll create this one." Before the angels fell, before time began, you were in the mind of God. Stop to think for a moment that God really designed you—decided that you would be, then waited for how long? Only Someone who truly loves you would wait that long for your appearance.

Spiritual Warfare

❖

Ephesians 6:10–18

S aint Paul says here, GROW STRONG IN THE LORD, WITH THE STRENGTH OF HIS POWER (6:10)—not my power, His power. PUT GOD'S ARMOUR ON (6:11).

Why are you supposed to grow strong in the Lord and why are you supposed to put on His power and His armor? SO AS TO BE ABLE TO RESIST THE DEVIL'S TACTICS (6:11). FOR IT IS NOT AGAINST HUMAN ENEMIES THAT WE HAVE TO STRUGGLE, BUT AGAINST THE SOVEREIGNTIES AND THE POWERS WHO ORIGINATE THE DARKNESS IN THIS WORLD, THE SPIRITUAL ARMY OF EVIL IN THE HEAVENS (6:12).

So STAND YOUR GROUND, WITH TRUTH BUCKLED ROUND YOUR WAIST (6:14). Do you understand? You cannot resist the enemy without the Lord. You cannot be strong without the Lord. You cannot do anything without the Lord. We're all different—kind of like a sassafras tree. Sassafras trees have different leaves. One looks like a glove, one looks like a clenched fist, and one has a little thumb protruding from the side. They're all of the same tree, but have different forms. This to me is one of the best things to analyze: to look at the diversity in God's Kingdom. Even though we are all pummeled by the enemy, the flesh, and the world (mostly the flesh), the solution for each of us is the same: God. In other words, we all come from the same tree, and the tree is God.

As we strive for holiness, all we have to say is yes to God, and He does it all. He does it all. We MUST RELY, he said, ON GOD'S ARMOUR (6:13). See, that's the freedom He wants for all of us. As I enjoy poor health—and I do enjoy it—it's a marvel to me that since I laid down and said, "Lord, if this is all You want for me to do at this point, it's all I need to do"—I've never seen so many wonderful fruits and so many wonderful things happen.

Saint Paul tells us to put on INTEGRITY FOR A BREASTPLATE (6:14), WEARING FOR SHOES ON YOUR FEET THE EAGERNESS TO SPREAD THE GOSPEL OF PEACE (6:15)—Zeal, Zeal—AND ALWAYS CARRYING THE SHIELD OF FAITH SO THAT YOU CAN USE IT TO PUT OUT THE BURNING ARROWS OF THE EVIL ONE (6:16). Faith actually counters the temptations and lures of the devil. Pretty good.

We've got to keep fighting. The only people who don't get anything accomplished or don't feel anything are mummies, but as long as you're breathing there is something happening in your soul. You're either going up or down. There's no way you can remain in the same place. In this struggle, you have to fight to keep moving upward. That's what we have to re-member. As we struggle for holiness, without any consolations, we often don't have the slightest idea that we're being trans-formed by God. But that is what's happening. You don't get a report card in the spiritual life, you get pain and sufferings and temptations. That's the report card. And it says: "You're making progress."

AND THEN YOU MUST ACCEPT SALVATION FROM GOD TO BE YOUR HELMET AND RECEIVE THE WORD OF GOD FROM THE SPIRIT TO USE AS A SWORD (6:17)—to fight back. And then here's the clincher: PRAY ALL THE TIME (6:18). All the time. How do you pray all the time?

Saint Paul says to PRAY ALL THE TIME, ASKING FOR WHAT YOU NEED (6:18). How do you like those apples? ASKING FOR WHAT YOU NEED (6:18). Sometimes we think of that as a kind of infe-rior prayer, like vocal prayer—petition prayer. In a petition we say, "Lord, please give me what I need." So let's try to put that into practice here and see what the Lord is saying. How many times do we say, "Lord, help me do something I do every day?"

What a prayer, to say, "Lord, at this meal let me not sin with my tongue." "Help me to have patience with my children at this event." "Lord, keep me from slugging this man." See, I can go from exercise to exercise, from event to event and never talk to the Lord in the course of the day. Saint Paul instructs us to keep PRAYING IN THE SPIRIT ON EVERY POSSIBLE OCCASION (6:18). Saint Paul is telling us how to pray without ceasing, how the Lord wants us to pray. To pray in the Spirit is to pray as the apostles prayed.

Praying in the spirit is to pray with the mind of Jesus. Saint Paul's talking about spiritual warfare. He wants our hearts and minds to be aligned with God's will. It means that I am open on every possible occasion, open to the power of God. That's the most important interpretation. To pray in the Spirit is to pray with the mind of God, to pray in love, out of love, to pray with the same will as the Father, and to pray with the same mind as the Father. On every possible occasion, pray that way.

NEVER GET TIRED OF STAYING AWAKE TO PRAY FOR ALL THE SAINTS (6:18). Pray for each other. Pray for the world. Pray for the Church. Pray for priests. Pray for religious. Pray for all those in cults, and all those Christians who have lost their faith. We've got so much to pray for. Ask the Lord for His help throughout your daily activities. When you do that you are saying, "Lord, I need You. I can't do anything without You. I can't make a recipe. I can't get to work. I can't answer the door or the phone. I can't do anything unless I get Your help." I assure you the Holy Spirit will rush to your aid. As the Lord said to Nicodemus of the Spirit, THE WIND BLOWS WHEREVER IT PLEASES. . . . YOU CANNOT TELL WHERE IT COMES FROM OR WHERE IT IS GOING (Jn 3:8).

The Behavior of a Christian and Discovering God's Will

❖

Romans 12:1–20

The following excerpt is fascinating. In addition to sharing her great insights on Saint Paul's letter to the Romans, Mother reveals a biographical detail that I had never seen before. She has often told this story from her childhood, but the detail here is arresting in its own right. As with Saint Paul, Mother's personal reference only sweetens the teaching.

Saint Paul writes in Romans: THINK OF GOD'S MERCY, MY BROTHERS, AND WORSHIP HIM, I BEG YOU, IN A WAY THAT IS WORTHY OF THINKING BEINGS, BY OFFERING YOUR LIVING BODIES AS A HOLY SACRIFICE, TRULY PLEASING TO GOD (12:1). Which means that we should give God whatever comes our way whether it's dry hair, or pimply skin, or a headache, a toothache, or just the weather—little things, not big things, but give Him a lot of little things.

DO NOT MODEL YOURSELVES ON THE BEHAVIOUR OF THE WORLD AROUND YOU, BUT LET YOUR BEHAVIOUR CHANGE, MODELLED BY YOUR NEW MIND (12:2). So Saint Paul was telling the Christians that they couldn't even think the way they used to think. They had to think differently. We have to examine ourselves once in a while, take an inventory of where we are and adjust the way we think. I don't know if you examine your conscience before your night prayers, but you should.

THIS IS THE ONLY WAY TO DISCOVER THE WILL OF GOD (12:2). Now isn't that kind of a switch. You'd think you'd discover the will of God first and then practice virtue. Well, here he's saying you practice virtue and THEN you'll discover the will of God. That's a real switch. That's something entirely different. We often pray that we may know the will of God. But it is only in accepting the opportunity of the present moment (whether it be one of joy or sorrow) that we begin to know the will of God for us. By looking for Jesus in the present moment, searching for Him in the occassions of our lives, we can begin to understand the will of God.

Let me read that again. LET YOUR BEHAVIOUR CHANGE, MODELLED ON YOUR NEW MIND. THIS IS THE ONLY WAY TO DISCOVER THE WILL OF GOD AND KNOW WHAT IS GOOD, WHAT IT IS THAT GOD WANTS, WHAT IS THE PERFECT THING TO DO (12:2). It's an amazing paragraph. The Scripture is filled, filled with short paragraphs that boggle your mind, and this is one of them. By not modeling myself on the behavior of the world, not thinking as the world thinks, but by changing my behavior, modeled by my new mind, I can discover the will of God. I can know what is good, I can know what God wants, and I can know the perfect thing to do. My Lord, that's a revelation.

See, we've got it twisted around. We think, "I must first know what God wants, know the perfect thing to do, then I can practice this virtue." Saint Paul is saying just the opposite. He says, "When my behavior's like Jesus's, then I know the will of God and what He wants and what the perfect thing to do is." So many people seek the will of God. What God has permitted in this present moment is His will. You only discover it after you have done it.

IN THE LIGHT OF THE GRACE I HAVE RECEIVED I WANT TO URGE EACH ONE AMONG YOU NOT TO EXAGGERATE HIS REAL IM-PORTANCE (12:3). Somebody somewhere was kind of strutting his Christianity around and Saint Paul was saying, "Lay off it. You're not that important."

I remember once I was given this award, the Mercy Award in Toledo, Ohio. There were about two thousand people at this luncheon. For some reason or other, it took four people to introduce me. The man introduced me and then the head of the organization introduced me, then some Sister came up and introduced me, and as I was listening to all these intro-ductions and all these compliments and so forth, I looked out among the tables and all the people, and suddenly the whole thing disappeared right in front of my eyes. It was as if the whole room was suddenly emptied. And I saw an incident in my mind's eye. I must have been eleven years old. I saw myself in bed with my mother. She was sound asleep. I saw the one-room apartment we were in. The whole thing became very real again. I was on my right side facing the wall. We used to hear rats gnawing at the floorboards at night. This one little guy had been gnawing for days and finally he got through—and I saw this rat. You know, rats are like little raccoons—they're big with long tails. And this guy came up and was scurrying on the floor. Well, I looked at him, and my heart stopped beating. I was petrified. I was cold all of a sudden. What was scary was he stopped in the middle of the floor, turned, and looked right at me. I thought for sure he'd jump because those rats will eat anything and he was obviously hungry. I was petrified. But he just looked at me and turned around and went his way. There was a door in our apartment that led to a room where the apartment owners used to keep garbage. The door didn't fit, and the rat squeezed himself under that door and left. This whole scene appeared to me while these people were giving me all these accolades and compliments.

I knew what the Lord was doing. I don't know whether I had begun to believe what they were saying, or whether the Lord wanted to remind me that whatever had been accomplished was from Him—but I got the point anyway. That little moment brought to mind what Saint Paul said, "Don't exaggerate your real importance because you have to judge yourself soberly by the standard of faith." I have to judge myself and examine my conscience by the standard of faith. How do I measure up to the standard of faith? How does my conduct measure up to the standard of faith?

JUST AS EACH OF OUR BODIES HAS SEVERAL PARTS AND EACH PART HAS A SEPARATE FUNCTION (12:4), SO ALL OF US, IN UNION WITH CHRIST, FORM ONE BODY, AND AS PARTS OF IT WE BELONG TO EACH OTHER (12:5). We are truly one body. We all have different functions, and we all represent different parts of this one body, but we're one body. We belong to each other. Our gifts differ according to the grace given us, but we are a crucial part of the whole.

DO NOT LET YOUR LOVE BE A PRETENCE, BUT SINCERELY PREFER GOOD TO EVIL (12:9). LOVE EACH OTHER AS MUCH AS BROTHERS SHOULD, AND HAVE A PROFOUND RESPECT FOR EACH OTHER (12:10). We have to learn to respect each other's very different personalities, different gifts, different ideals and ideas. We have to respect those differences as something beautiful, and God given.

IF YOU HAVE HOPE, THIS WILL MAKE YOU CHEERFUL. DO NOT GIVE UP IF TRIALS COME; AND KEEP ON PRAYING (12:12). Sometimes we forget that. We don't keep on praying. And IF ANY OF THE SAINTS ARE IN NEED YOU MUST SHARE WITH THEM; AND YOU SHOULD MAKE HOSPITALITY YOUR SPECIAL CARE (12:13). That's why when people come to visit, we must be hospitable. They must always feel that they're not only welcome, but we're happy to see them. I think that's such a great thing because people see and feel our joy. Elsewhere in the Scripture it says: we must be hospitable because some people entertain angels as Abraham did (Heb 13:2).

I would advise you to read Romans chapter 12 because it has an awful lot of goodies in it. BLESS THOSE WHO PERSECUTE YOU: NEVER CURSE THEM, BLESS THEM (12:14). REJOICE WITH THOSE WHO REJOICE AND BE SAD WITH THOSE IN SORROW (12:15). TREAT EVERYONE WITH EQUAL KINDNESS; NEVER BE CONDESCENDING BUT MAKE REAL FRIENDS WITH THE POOR. DO NOT ALLOW YOURSELF TO BECOME SELF-SATISFIED (12:16). Never think that you've done enough, or you've worked hard enough, or you've been kind enough. NEVER REPAY EVIL WITH EVIL BUT LET EVERYONE SEE THAT YOU ARE INTERESTED ONLY IN

THE HIGHEST IDEALS (12:17). DO ALL YOU CAN TO LIVE AT PEACE WITH EVERYONE (12:18). NEVER TRY TO GET REVENGE; LEAVE THAT, MY FRIENDS, TO GOD'S ANGER (12:19).

Paul is kind of funny, he doesn't believe in exacting revenge on your enemies, but he has a quotation here that is classic. He says, Vengeance is mine—I WILL PAY THEM BACK, THE LORD PROMISES (12:19). . . . IF YOUR ENEMY IS HUNGRY, YOU SHOULD GIVE HIM FOOD, AND IF HE IS THIRSTY, LET HIM DRINK. THUS YOU HEAP RED-HOT COALS ON HIS HEAD (12:20). I think that's the funniest line in Scirpture. So being nice to your enemy, you heap red-hot coals on his head. We can try to make something nice out of it, but somehow I think he meant red-hot coals! Oh well.

Mother's Favorite Line in Scripture

❖

2 Corinthians 3:18; Assorted

Saint Paul's epistles are a theology of the spiritual life, a theology of Christianity. You can't read Saint Paul's epistles for even a moment without realizing that he is talking about living in holiness and charity (to the Thessalonians), explaining Christian behavior, and warning against errors (in Colossians).

In Second Corinthians, Saint Paul speaks a lot about our human nature. He says, TO STOP ME FROM GETTING TOO PROUD I WAS GIVEN A THORN IN THE FLESH (2 Cor 12:7). There's no human being in the whole wide world who does not have a thorn in their flesh. There's one weak spot in your spiritual life, in your nature, in your soul that is like an internal Achilles' heel. We all have one. Paul says, I HAVE PLEADED WITH THE LORD THREE TIMES FOR IT TO LEAVE ME (12:8), BUT HE HAS SAID, "MY

GRACE IS ENOUGH FOR YOU: MY POWER IS AT ITS BEST IN WEAK-NESS" (2 Cor 12:9). This is a concept lost on the world. That's why I encourage you to read the epistles so often. God says, "MY POWER IS AT ITS BEST IN WEAKNESS." And a typical Saint Paul remark is I AM QUITE CONTENT WITH MY WEAKNESSES (2 Cor 12:10). We must embrace that weakness, embrace that cross and let God transform it.

Paul speaks in Second Corinthians about the ultimate in transforming union. The ultimate. AND WE, WITH OUR UNVEILED FACES REFLECTING LIKE MIRRORS THE BRIGHTNESS OF THE LORD, ALL GROW BRIGHTER AND BRIGHTER AS WE ARE TURNED INTO THE IMAGE THAT WE REFLECT; THIS IS THE WORK OF THE LORD WHO IS SPIRIT (2 Cor 3:18). That's my favorite line in Scripture.

In another translation it reads: BUT WE ALL BEHOLDING THE GLORY OF THE LORD WITH OPEN FACE, ARE TRANSFORMED INTO THE SAME IMAGE FROM GLORY TO GLORY AS BY THE SPIRIT OF THE LORD (3:18).

Our lives have to reflect something of Jesus. You know, each of us is attracted to a different aspect of Our Lord's life. Some are attracted to His ministry, some are attracted to His Sacred Heart, the gentleness of Jesus, His compassion, His strength, His mercy, His patience. We all have something or some aspect of Our Lord's life that we're attracted to. And if we're attracted to it, we try to reflect it. We have to know that even the holiest of us is a mere reflection.

Now, is that all we are, reflections? Are we just here to REFLECT LIKE MIRRORS THE BRIGHTNESS OF THE LORD? No. We ALL GROW BRIGHTER AND BRIGHTER. And that's what the contemplative life is supposed to accomplish. We not only grow bright but we grow brighter and brighter. For what reason? To be TURNED INTO THE IMAGE THAT WE REFLECT (3:18). So it is not just an image we reveal to others; we're supposed to be turned *into* that image.

The other day I was reading about a favorite saint of mine. During the canonization process, people were asked to come and share their recollections of him. A peasant came forward and said, "I went to see a man, but I saw God." This is exactly what Saint Paul is talking about. We should reflect like a mirror the brightness of the Lord. But you can't do that if you're not totally obsessed with accomplishing the will of God and practicing love and charity. Charity is different from love. Ordinary love is my love for you. Charity is my love for God.

Remember, what we do is of no consequence, what we accomplish is of no consequence if our hearts, our souls, our bodies, our minds, our spirits are not being transformed. And the only way to transformation, the only way to reflect the "brightness of the Lord" is to hug the cross. In the spiritual life sometimes you're searching and searching for something you already possess. We look for holiness, but we rebel against the cross. We don't want dryness of spirit, soul, and mind. We don't want to go through that desolation or crisis or loss. We want holiness, but we don't want to spend time in prayer, and we don't want to keep our minds straight and clear and occupied with the Lord alone. See, I think that somewhere along the line we feel that holiness is a gift from God that requires nothing of us—that you wake up one morning and presto! You're suddenly holy. Sorry. It takes a lot of guts, guts right down here in your stomach, and it takes a lot of effort, and a tremendous amount of grace and emptying of self to achieve holiness. What must we rid ourselves of to permit God entry into our lives? Identify those thorns in your flesh and let God help you overcome them. In the doing, you'll find holiness.

A Life of Love

❖

2 John 1:4–6

I n the Second Epistle of Saint John, the very short one, he
says, IT HAS GIVEN ME GREAT JOY TO FIND THAT YOUR CHIL-
DREN HAVE BEEN LIVING THE LIFE OF TRUTH AS WE WERE COM-
MANDED BY THE FATHER (1:4). AND I AM WRITING NOW . . . NOT
TO GIVE YOU ANY NEW COMMANDMENT, BUT THE ONE WHICH WE
WERE GIVEN AT THE BEGINNING, AND TO PLEAD: LET US LOVE
ONE ANOTHER (1:5). It would be wonderful if we would remember this commandment of the Lord. If we did, the Lord would
be so much within us, and we so united to Him. We would be
able to live this commandment, and live it in such a way that
everyone would know that we are Christians.

I read a line the other day and it said, "If you were jailed
because you were a Christian, would they have enough evidence to convict you?" And I wonder how many of us would
display enough evidence that we are Christians to be convicted
in a court. Do our daily actions and our way of life demonstrate
to people that we are Christians?

Then Saint John says, TO LOVE IS TO LIVE ACCORDING TO
HIS COMMANDMENT: THIS IS THE COMMANDMENT WHICH YOU
HAVE HEARD SINCE THE BEGINNING, TO LIVE A LIFE OF LOVE
(1:6). To live a life of love. Perhaps the reason the world has
grown cold is that Christianity has become just a code of eth-
ics and not a way of life. Our lives are no longer a way of love.
We are kind to people because it seems to be the thing to

do. But we do not love them as the Master loves us, and we should—no—we must.

A Last Warning

❖

Jude 1:3–23

S aint Jude only has one epistle, but he had the same problem that Paul and Timothy and Peter had. No matter where the apostles went it seems someone came behind them and sowed bad seed. Jude says that he had been wanting to write for a long time and that we must FIGHT HARD FOR THE FAITH WHICH HAS BEEN ONCE AND FOR ALL ENTRUSTED TO THE SAINTS (1:3). A real Christian is a saint—the two words should be synonymous. We shouldn't think of saints as just wonder-workers. Those are charisms, but it has nothing to do with faith or sanctity.

Jude says, CERTAIN PEOPLE HAVE INFILTRATED AMONG YOU, AND THEY ARE THE ONES YOU HAD A WARNING ABOUT, IN WRIT-ING, LONG AGO, WHEN THEY WERE CONDEMNED FOR DENYING ALL RELIGION, TURNING THE GRACE OF OUR GOD INTO IMMO-RALITY (1:4). They had the same problem we have today: the love bit. Everything is love, love, love. As long as it is "love," there is no sin. You just need to love, that's all. They turned the grace of God into immorality and used love as an excuse to do what they pleased, when they pleased.

Saint Jude reminds his readers of THE ANGELS WHO HAD SUPREME AUTHORITY BUT DID NOT KEEP IT AND LEFT THEIR AP-POINTED SPHERE; HE HAS KEPT THEM DOWN IN THE DARK, IN SPIRITUAL CHAINS, TO BE JUDGED ON THE GREAT DAY (1:6). He brings up the fall of the angels: creatures who had fantastic light and pure intelligence—and they fell. We too can fall. This is a warning so that we do not become self-sufficient and arrogant. He continues: THE FORNICATION OF SODOM AND GOMORRAH AND THE OTHER NEARBY TOWNS WAS EQUALLY UN-NATURAL, AND IT IS A WARNING TO US THAT THEY ARE PAYING FOR THEIR CRIMES IN ETERNAL FIRE (1:7). We are not dealing with a vengeful God who condemns people to hell. Everyone who goes to hell wants to go. Hell is a choice you make. It is a total rejection of God and His love—and once you reject God's love there is only hate.

He says later: THESE PEOPLE ARE (1:8) . . . LIKE UNREA-SONING ANIMALS (1:10) . . . THEY ARE LIKE CLOUDS BLOWN ABOUT BY THE WINDS AND BRINGING NO RAIN, OR LIKE BARREN TREES WHICH ARE UPROOTED IN THE WINTER . . . TWICE DEAD (1:12); . . . LIKE SHOOTING STARS BOUND FOR ETERNITY OF BLACK DARKNESS (1:13). It is strange that men who were with the gentle Christ for three years, men who preached love, who performed beautiful miracles, had to be hard at times. And Saint Jude is being hard here. He is trying to awaken us to the reality of evil in the world, warning us that there are people who will destroy your faith if you allow them to. We too must discern when it is time to be hard, to be tough with ourselves and others.

Then Jude goes on: REMEMBER, MY DEAR FRIENDS, WHAT THE APOSTLES OF OUR LORD JESUS CHRIST TOLD YOU TO EXPECT (1:17). "AT THE END OF TIME," THEY TOLD YOU[,] "THERE ARE GO-ING TO BE PEOPLE WHO SNEER AT RELIGION AND FOLLOW NOTH-ING BUT THEIR OWN DESIRES FOR WICKEDNESS" (1:18). THESE UNSPIRITUAL AND SELFISH PEOPLE ARE NOTHING BUT MISCHIEF-MAKERS (1:19). Now the apostles thought they were at the end of time, as every generation since them has believed. Since Christ, every generation has looked for His Second Coming. There will be a generation that will see it. Take a look around:

never have so many people sneered at religion as they do today. The mischief makers are everywhere.

Jude then says: BUT YOU, MY DEAR FRIENDS, MUST USE YOUR MOST HOLY FAITH AS YOUR FOUNDATION AND BUILD ON THAT, PRAYING TO THE HOLY SPIRIT (1:20); KEEP YOURSELVES WITHIN THE LOVE OF GOD AND WAIT FOR THE MERCY OF OUR LORD JESUS CHRIST TO GIVE YOU ETERNAL LIFE (1:21). WHEN THERE ARE SOME WHO HAVE DOUBTS, REASSURE THEM (1:22); WHEN THERE ARE SOME TO BE SAVED FROM THE FIRE, PULL THEM OUT; BUT THERE ARE OTHERS TO WHOM YOU MUST BE KIND WITH GREAT CAUTION, KEEPING YOUR DISTANCE EVEN FROM OUTSIDE CLOTHING WHICH IS CONTAMINATED BY VICE (1:23). I marvel sometimes at the whole-sale evil in the world today. Today we like to test ourselves by putting ourselves in the middle of the fire, in the presence of sin. The evil one uses scandal in other people's lives to ruin your faith and you cannot let that happen. You cannot let your faith rely on people, or churches, or ministers, but on God. People will disap-point you, but His Word and His Church will not.

Mother Angelica's Advice for Examining Your Conscience

❖

Before we go, let's talk a little bit about examination of con-science. I think it's necessary every night, or every after-noon if you wish, to examine your conscience. Examination of conscience should not be something picky; it is not to en-courage scrupulosity. This examination is simply an exercise to clean this dish, this earthenware jar, our souls, inside and out—just as you would clean anything else. I don't think too many of you go without taking a bath every day; at least I hope you don't. But we allow our souls to get full of dust, full of cobwebs, full of all kinds of dirt.

The examination of conscience should be very calm, and conducted at a time of day when you have a moment to reflect—and be extremely honest. Do it in your room at night. You can't do it in the morning because you're just getting started, and in the afternoon you've got a long way to go. It's a time when you should look at yourself objectively, almost as a third person. That's the best way to do it, without providing any reasons and excuses. Simply say: *I did this.* It doesn't matter who enticed you to do it; it doesn't matter whether the occasion was just or unjust—none of that matters. *I did this thing: "I was unloving, I was unkind, I was impatient, I was angry, I was lustful, I showed disgust, or I showed annoyance. I committed these things, and I missed these opportunities."*

We should just sit before the Lord and say interiorly, *"Lord, what did I do today that was not pleasing to You?"* Leave everybody out of your examination of conscience. Forget saying: *"I don't like Mike, or I'm jealous of Sally"*—that is of no concern, because at death the Lord isn't going to ask you one thing about Mike, about your family, about your relatives, or Sally. He'll want to know what *you* did.

It's extremely important that you make an examination of conscience every day, no matter how brief, and keep your neighbor out of it. If you're honest with Him, you'll find yourself less and less disturbed with everybody else. It should sound something like this:

Lord, I was rotten today. I was arrogant, I was proud, I was impatient, I was unloving, I was unkind. I was not obedient in my mind; I was obedient in action but I missed being obedient in my reason. I missed so many opportunities today, Lord. I missed occasions of grace, Lord. I did not forgive readily. I was not thoughtful today. I was not able to overcome myself. I was cruel to a coworker. I was disinterested in what my wife said this morning at breakfast. I lied to get out of the dinner early so I wouldn't have to see that woman. I am constantly making excuses, Lord. Forgive me. Help me.

You see, with an examination like that, you give it all to the Lord. And after you say it, you forget it, like you do in confession. Say, *"Lord, I'm sorry for all of this, and I do most of this out of pride, and I'm going to try harder tomorrow."* You put it to rest. You bury it; it's gone now. You've had the courage to admit *you* are the one at fault. There's nobody else but you. It's very important that you do this every day. It's a cleansing of the soul. It's not a replacement for confession, because your sins are not forgiven, but it makes you more sensitive to the root causes of sin. It's kind of like a daily spiritual checkup.

Without an examination of conscience every day, I don't know how you can sincerely progress in the spiritual life, because if you don't know what's wrong with you, how are you going to improve? If you just eat, sleep, drink, pray, and thoughtlessly go to bed at night, how are you ever going to know yourself? How will you know what part of you is not like the Lord? Be very honest, my friends.

You know what's so strange? I find that some Sisters who very rarely make an examination of conscience refuse to be honest even when they're alone. Some laypeople probably have the same problem. Do they think they're kidding God? You were a louse all day long. You may as well admit it. When we're dealing with the Lord, we need to be totally transparent. And although we think everybody and his uncle are the cause of our transgressions, it is not true. They are merely occasions.

You can't go to heaven disliking even one person. Oh, dear Lord. Now, unless we overcome that totally and really love everybody, we're going to spend some time in purgatory.

Saint Paul brings out this point beautifully: YOU ARE GOD'S CHOSEN RACE, HIS SAINTS; HE LOVES YOU, AND YOU SHOULD BE CLOTHED IN SINCERE COMPASSION, IN KINDNESS AND HUMILITY, GENTLENESS AND PATIENCE (Col 3:12).

You ought to type this out and keep it in your pocket: Colossians 3:12–17. It's a wonderful examination of conscience. Paul goes on: BEAR WITH ONE ANOTHER; FORGIVE EACH OTHER AS SOON AS A QUARREL BEGINS—because, he says, THE LORD HAS FORGIVEN YOU, NOW YOU MUST DO THE SAME (3:13). OVER ALL THESE CLOTHES, TO KEEP THEM TOGETHER AND COMPLETE THEM, PUT ON LOVE (3:14). It's an awesome little paragraph. First of all it tells you who you are, what you are, and then it tells you how to change it. AND MAY THE PEACE OF CHRIST REIGN IN YOUR HEARTS . . . That's another little examination of conscience: Does the peace of Jesus reign in your heart? In heaven it has to, all the time. You must have the kind of humility to know you're not God's gift to humanity, never were and never will be—unless you become a great saint. That's your only value: You've got to be what God wants you to be.

Now go down to the next verse: LET THE MESSAGE OF CHRIST, IN ALL ITS RICHNESS, FIND A HOME IN YOU. TEACH EACH OTHER, AND ADVISE EACH OTHER, IN ALL WISDOM. Most of the time we only chitchat about incidentals, our faults and weaknesses. But we should be teaching each other, advising each other. WITH GRATITUDE IN YOUR HEARTS SING PSALMS AND HYMNS AND INSPIRED SONGS TO GOD (3:16). That doesn't mean you've got to sing out loud, God help us all . . . AND NEVER SAY OR DO ANYTHING EXCEPT IN THE NAME OF THE LORD JESUS. So, can you say all the things you say in front of Him? In His name? And finally, give THANKS TO GOD THE FATHER THROUGH HIM (3:17).

Here you've got an entire examination of conscience, the solution, and you have the reason—peace of heart.

You could concentrate on these few lines for the rest of your life. This examination of conscience could be the very best. It gives you light, it gives you hope, and you see the end of the tunnel, but it's realistic and it doesn't pat you on the back. And don't forget: if you have to forgive your neighbor, you also have to forgive yourself.

Use this time of examination to thank God for the occasions when you did come up to par. *"Lord, I thank You that I didn't sock Frank right in the kisser. I felt like it, but I didn't do it, and I thank You for that grace. I thank You for the chance to go on for another hour and maintain my composure, because I was so tired today. I thank You for that."* See, that's honesty. It's so critical that you perform a daily, honest to goodness evaluation of your miserable day. If you do that, tomorrow will be a lot less miserable, and so will you.

FINAL PRAYER

Lord God, I ask pardon for all our sins.

Lord, for all the times we've offended You in thought,

word, or deed;

for the selfishness in our lives and the ego that blocks

You out of our minds and hearts.

I ask pardon for the distractions that keep

leading us away from You.

I ask for Your mercy upon us, and on the whole world.

Prepare our hearts and minds, Lord, for what is to come.

Prepare our souls, our thoughts, our will, and give us strength

to fight the good fight. Give us communal love, Lord,

the kind that will bind us together as one in the heart of Jesus.

We ask, Lord, small and insignificant as we are,

that we may give You comfort and love.

We ask for pardon, Lord, for those who crown You with thorns by

their pride and arrogance. We ask pardon for those who scourge

You at the pillar by their immorality.

Lord, we ask pardon for those who strip You of your garments

by their greed and ambition for worldly things.

We ask pardon for all mankind. We ask pardon,

Lord, for the whole world, for all of our sins.

Be merciful to us, Lord. We praise and glorify Your name,

for You are holy, You alone.

We glorify Your justice, Lord, and Your mercy.

We praise and bless You.

Amen.

Acknowledgments

❖

I must first thank the woman who spent much of her life speaking the truths assembled on these pages. Today, even hidden in the silence of her monastery in Hanceville, Alabama, Mother Mary Angelica continues to spend long hours with her spouse, interceding for her spiritual children around the world. And though she is no doubt still seeing "invisible things" and hearing "unutterable words," she can no longer share them with us as she once did. Today she reflects what she has beheld. I am thankful to her for her prayers, her example, and for her continuing affection. This and the two books that preceded it are small tokens of my gratitude.

There is no way I could have assembled this book without the martyrlike labors of Sister Maria Consolata PCPA of Our Lady of the Angels Monastery. Sister spent many weeks transferring Mother's lessons from disintegrating audiotapes. She not only saved these priceless teachings; she then carefully transcribed them along with Sister Mary Paschal PCPA. The good cheer and humor of Sister Consolata never flagged, nor did her ability to locate just the right lesson for me. Sister Grace Marie PCPA has my appreciation for the splendid shot she snapped of Mother, which truly *made* the cover of this book. I am also thankful to the vicar of Our Lady of the Angels Monastery, Sister Mary Catherine PCPA who has been a constant encouragement and a wonderful collaborator. For their continuing prayers, I thank all of Mother's Sisters, some of whom are now relocated to foundations in France, Arizona, Ohio, and elsewhere.

There are so many people I have to thank for sustaining me through yet another book. First, there is my wife, Rebecca, and our children: Alexander, Lorenzo, and Mariella. They sacrificed so many nights and weekends for this work, allowing me to hide out in my office, litter the kitchen table, or run to the coffee shop to complete it. The process of assembling a collection like this is long and arduous, but my family was always there to bolster the editor. Any success this work enjoys is the direct result of their love and support. They are the animating spirit that gives me meaning, and my greatest hope for the future. I love you all so very much.

There are also many dear friends to whom I am indebted for their persistent devotion and encouragement: Christopher Edwards, my steadfast producer and wing man, who is always there; Doug Keck, my long-suffering executive producer; Laura Ingraham, one of the few people who never fails to send me into hysterics, even when her dog is devouring my chair; Michael Paternostro; Jim Caviezel; Umberto and Maryellen Fedeli; Andrew T. Miller; Ron Hansen; Kate O'Beirne; Carl Amari; and Joseph Looney. Your friendship means more to me than you know.

At EWTN I am grateful to James Faulkner, Lee South, Peter Gagnon, Michael Warsaw, and Bill Steltemeier for keeping Mother and her editor on the air.

At Doubleday my editor Trace Murphy has done it again. He has been there for all three of the Mother Angelica books, displaying his usual great taste and kindness throughout. Thank you, Trace. For his steady support of my efforts, the president of Doubleday, Steve Rubin, has my gratitude and esteem. For bringing me to Doubleday, I need to thank Michelle Rapkin, my first publisher—and for making me feel at home, I thank her successor, the brass-tacks visionary Bill Barry. Bill made sure that my work was everywhere, and beat the drum until the audience took notice. He is the best there is.

Then there are special people who have assisted me in ways I could never thank them enough for: my fearless agent Loretta Barrett is always in my corner, and her crew Nick Mullendore and Gabriel Davis are simply incredible; Greg Mueller and Peter Robbio of Creative Response Concepts, as well as Cari Beckman publicized my work like no one could. They are miracle workers all.

And finally there is you. But for your attention and commitment, Mother's full story would still be untold and her best lessons would be confined to her monastery archive. I am so thankful for you, my literary and broadcast family, who continue to support my work. Thank you for being there, and I promise to keep bringing you work that inspires and challenges . . . so stay tuned.

Doubleday kindly allowed me to quote from the 1966 edition of their *Jerusalem Bible*. It is Mother Angelica's favorite Bible, and the one she used for all her scriptural teachings, both on air and off.